ƒP

FLIP
THE
SCRIPT

How to Turn the Tables and Win in Business and Life

BILL WACKERMANN

FREE PRESS
New York   London   Toronto   Sydney   New Delhi

fP

Free Press
A Division of Simon & Schuster, Inc.
1230 Avenue of the Americas
New York, NY 10020

First Free Press hardcover edition May 2012

FREE PRESS and colophon are trademarks of Simon & Schuster, Inc.

For information about special discounts for bulk purchases,
please contact Simon & Schuster Special Sales at
1-866-506-1949 or business@simonandschuster.com.

The Simon & Schuster Speakers Bureau can bring authors to your
live event. For more information or to book an event contact the
Simon & Schuster Speakers Bureau at 1-866-248-3049
or visit our website at www.simonspeakers.com.

Designed by Julie Schroeder

Manufactured in the United States of America

1 3 5 7 9 10 8 6 4 2

Library of Congress Cataloging-in-Publication Data
Wackermann, Bill.
Flip the script: how to turn the tables and win in business
and life / Bill Wackermann
p. cm.
Includes bibliographical references and index.
1. Success in business. 2. Success. 3. Life skills. I. Title.
HF5386.W14 2012
650.1—dc23   2011038892

ISBN 978-1-4516-1839-6
ISBN 978-1-4516-1842-6 (ebook)

For Theodore, Hugh, and Helena

Anything is possible.

CONTENTS

PREFACE

I have read many books on how to succeed in business, and often, after reading them, I have been left wondering if the authors' own experiences were relatable to the average person. The advice in many of the books tended to be either too scholarly or too complicated to incorporate into real life. The lack of a better-grounded, reality-based approach to guiding others to success inspired me to think about my own experiences.

My success in life and business has come in the absence of any extraordinary opportunity or vision. Mine is a journey from a family of six children who struggled monthly to make ends meet to a career in one of publishing's glittering ivory towers. From New York to Paris, from the world of fashion and beauty to the back lots of Hollywood, my success has come from "flipping the script" and creating opportunities where none existed. Flipping the script is my unique approach to turning tables and gaining control.

I've found that there are certain principles and steps for transforming a business or turning your life around that are not difficult to follow and that work time and again. You'll find them to be of incredible value no matter where you come from, what school you attended, or where you are in your career. Throughout this book I will show you how to flip the script and use the simple and relatable core principles of this process to change your life for the better.

Growing up in a small working-class town on the eastern end of Long Island, my expectations for academic or professional achievement were not high. Middle Island was the type of place where no one special came from. And you never expected anyone would. Many of my peers' career prospects were realized after high school upon securing a good job at the telephone company or cutting hair three days a week at the local hair salon.

The town is seventy miles from New York City; that glittering beacon seems close, but it's another world. Middle Island is inhabited by decent, hardworking people for whom I have tremendous respect, but there is also much to be said about creating dreams that expand outside of the world and circumstances you are born into. No one prepares you for this. I've worked loading trucks, flipping burgers, and cleaning pools. I've also worked hand in hand with the world's glitterati. From fashion's heavyweights to Hollywood's biggest and most demanding players, I've used the principle of flipping to stand toe-to-toe with giants—and win.

Understanding how to create opportunity for myself was my ticket out, and learning the tools for rewriting my own script has kept me at the top of my industry. I'll draw upon all my experiences and endeavors to bring *Flip the Script* to life and show you exactly how this mind-set and approach play out in the real world. The first step is simple: embrace the notion that turning a situation around and creating new opportunities takes the desire to face yourself as you really are and a willingness to see the potential that could be hiding right in front of you.

Throughout this book, I'll share principles and rules for doing just this—and for rewriting the script of your life. The process boils down to three stages: (1) understanding yourself, (2) navigating how to build your flip, and (3) winning: overcoming obstacles and pulling it all together. Within these three stages are guiding principles and rules to help you learn how to get at the heart of what you want and remove the obstacles that stand in your way. Many times we put these obstacles up ourselves. Understanding how and why you think or behave the way you do is the first step to successfully flipping your script. I'll show you how to free your mind by embracing the power of "So what?" Understanding the power of "So what?" will help you realize that every problem has several solutions and can be overcome.

You will also learn to better control your irrational fears and gain a new sense of personal accountability so that you can stop blaming everyone else but you for your station in life.

With your newfound sense of self-awareness, you'll be ready to maneuver yourself into new opportunities—ethically, responsibly, and with a design toward sustained success. You'll figure out what changes are most important and needed in your life and map out a strategy for making them happen. Once you've set your sights on a goal or opportunity, there are effective ways of going after it that will add to your reputation and make achieving it much more doable. You'll read about these techniques in the last section of the book. There you'll find field-tested methods that can help you turn around any situation and take control. You'll be able to identify, through honest and sometimes funny real-life business and personal situations, how many of us struggle with the same issues and how you can learn to successfully navigate these challenges. The techniques offered in this book will put you in the winner's circle, whether that means breaking free of mediocre expectations or achieving at the highest level. It doesn't matter whether you are a recent grad starting out in your career, re-creating yourself after being downsized, or on the fast track to the executive floor; flipping is a way for you to realize your ambitions, because it encourages you to think that every problem or situation can be turned around for your benefit—and that you have the power to make it happen.

To bring these rules to life, I will share stories that are honest, self-revelatory, and humorous from my more than twenty years of turning businesses around. From one of the youngest magazine publishers to Sundance finalist film producer, I'm honored to share my keys for flipping with you. This book will be an invaluable guide for understanding how to become more effective in business and in life.

In the end, though, the real work is up to you. I will share stories, lessons learned, and tools to empower you, but in the end, as the last chapter says, it's up to you. These tools can and will work; flipping is achievable for everyone. It's a lesson that I'm fortunate to have discovered early in life. Let me tell you how it all started.

INTRODUCTION

When I first had the idea to write this book, I wondered, "Should I really be giving others advice, business or otherwise? I usually have more questions than answers." I also thought about the fact that all the so-called experts I'd known over the years had always seemed so smug and self-assured, so confident that their methods could fix whatever ailed anyone either in business or in life. Suffice it to say, I had my doubts about what I could contribute to the literature and the cacophony of voices that regularly chime in on the subject of how to succeed.

Let me begin by saying that I don't have all the answers—and I probably wouldn't believe anyone who says he or she does. No one can fix any problem in your life but *you.* Your success in doing that will be determined by how hard you are willing to look at yourself and your ability to deconstruct the patterns of behavior that you've established over a lifetime. In this endeavor, as someone who has climbed the corporate ladder from the bottom and fought rung by rung to make it to the top, I can be of help.

I can offer something simple yet effective: a philosophy and some easy rules that I have found to work for me as well as for my peers, colleagues, and friends. The premise of this book is rooted in a belief that you have to do the unexpected, that by taking a situation in which you feel you do not have control or options and establishing control—that is, by "flipping the script"—you can create options and make positive changes in both your professional and personal life.

WHAT IT MEANS TO FLIP THE SCRIPT

We all view ourselves as the star of our own movie, but too often we allow ourselves to think that the script and all of the action has already been written for us. We may feel that there is no way to turn a challenging business situation around, or we may be uncertain about how to improve our personal circumstances. Flipping the script is about truly seeing your real self, stripping away rationalizations and closely examining your limiting tendencies and bad habits, getting a sense of all your options, and then making choices freely. Flipping is liberating; in so doing, you write your own script. This allows you to be your best despite challenging circumstances, and it enables you to write new and exciting chapters in business and in life. Finally, flipping gives you the freedom to be nimble and to control the ending of your story.

ARE YOU READY FOR YOUR CLOSE-UP?

The first step you need to take in order to flip your scripts is to understand your true self. Psychologists say that an ever-increasing number of businesspeople today hold opinions of themselves that don't match how the world, their employers, their families, or their friends see them. As the British philosopher Bertrand Russell put it, "The trouble with the world is that the stupid are cocksure and the intelligent are full of doubt." So let me ask you, are you cocksure and foolish, or do you know the right answer but doubt your abilities? Either way, all of us have this kind of blindness to a certain degree, but take a close look at your life—are the blind spots keeping you from moving forward, getting a promotion, finding love in your life, or having better relationships with your coworkers, family, and friends? When you can't see yourself or your life clearly, how can you make accurate and thoughtful choices that will propel you forward?

A lack of self-awareness can be hysterically funny in fictional settings. This is often the main conceit in much of today's television programming. Steve Carell's character Michael Scott on *The Office* is an epic example of this; it's funny to watch him blindly offend his office mates. But is it as funny if you're the person feeling offended or are the one offending others? Similar examples of nonexistent self-awareness abound in pop culture; there's no better evidence of delusional behavior than the stars of reality shows. They seem to have little to no realization of how they are perceived by viewers. How else could anyone explain their outlandish, clueless, and self-destructive behavior? Though this makes for great television, it's not such a great way to behave in real life.

In real life this lack of awareness isn't funny or entertaining, and, more important, it can keep you from advancing in your career and from improving your personal relationships. Such blind spots are universal. The good news is that through understanding how to flip the script we can begin to see our true selves and minimize the negative impact of those blind spots. I like to think of the process of flipping as teaching yourself to hear your own voice. What I mean by that is that many times we have so much internal dialogue in our heads. Years of fear, psychological baggage, and insecurity fog our judgment so that we don't see our behavior or hear our "voice" with the clarity that others around us do. I hope that through the process of learning to flip you will begin to hear your own voice and see your own actions in your consciousness, in much the same way a video recorder would capture them. To illustrate my point, think about the fact that most people, when they're recorded and hear their voice or see their image on video, always seem to say similar things, such as "Do I really sound like that?" or "Did I really do that?" The answer is yes, you did, and not seeing yourself as others see you can cause blind spots that hold you back.

So what does it mean to flip? Flipping is about turning your expectations upside down. I can tell you that it's *not* about taking the expected route. Flipping is about being self-confident and strong, not allowing circumstances to manage you but rather finding the best way to manage any circumstance. Flipping means that you first have to face your fears, because what you fear controls you. Once you are no longer in the grip of fear, you'll be free to create innovative new patterns of behavior. Finally, flipping is about being flexible and open-minded, because anything can be flipped: an angry boss, a hostile negotiation, or a relationship headed in the wrong direction. We'll go through those scenarios later on in the book, and I'll show you the ways in which I and others have successfully flipped the script.

With that in mind, let me share with you the story of my first flip.

FLIPPING AT FOURTEEN

I really started to understand the power of flipping as a fourteen-year-old eighth grader. I was born the fifth of six children and raised in a lower-middle-income hamlet on Long Island. Despite, or possibly because of, the many distractions at home, I became a decent student. Achieving academically in elementary school had an added bonus in that it distinguished me from my older brothers and sisters. Seeing my aptitude for school, my mother wanted to nurture my academic inclinations, and although she was satisfied with the local elementary school, she feared that the local high school was too large and undisciplined a place for me. She was probably right to be concerned. The local high school, Longwood, was a product of one of the many educational misfires of the 1970s.

Longwood was like communism: a good idea that just didn't work in reality. Longwood was a spectacular building designed as a circular structure. It had no traditional classrooms or walls but instead featured open-air spaces with only midheight dividers to separate the classes. With no real walls to block out sound, students could hear every other class around them. Talk about distractions.

My mother worried that if I enrolled at Longwood, I would follow in the footsteps of several of my older siblings, who had attended the school with varying degrees of success. Though my eldest brother had done well, going to college and eventually law school, my other older siblings struggled.

In an effort to help me avoid the same fate, my mother planned to send me to a parochial high school in the hope that the strict rules and discipline would keep me focused. (She didn't know the essential irony of parochial school, which quickly became clear to me: Catholic school kids are the wildest.) After applying to several schools, we settled on St. John the Baptist. Located in West Islip, New York, St. John's was about an hour away from where we lived at the time. West Islip is an affluent beach community, so St. John's had been dubbed "Where the snobs meet the slobs." I was quick to learn that I was the latter.

As with most things in my family growing up, the plan was grand but only half baked. We thought nothing of applying to schools, going on interviews, and accepting enrollment—all without ever figuring out how we would pay the $1,500 yearly tuition. In addition, the school was more than an hour away, and my father took the one car my family had to work every day. So basically, I was accepted at a school for which we had no money for me to attend and no way to get me there and back. I was presented with the perfect opportunity to enact my very first flip.

FIGURING IT OUT

As the excitement of acceptance wore off, I asked my mother, "Can you afford this? And, by the way, how will I get there and back every day?" The impact of her response was nothing short of monumental; it shaped every aspect of my life then—and now. She said, "Well, I guess you are just going to have to figure it out." Me? What was I supposed to do? I was fourteen! The idea that I should figure it out was a very empowering, though completely frightening, concept for a fourteen-year-old. "Figuring it out" meant "I don't have the answer today, but let's proceed as if we do." Another way to think about this concept is what I call positive projecting, the belief that things will work out in your favor, even though you can't see exactly how at the current time.

To put the money together for the tuition, I decided I'd have to take several summer jobs, mowing lawns and doing odd jobs to help my parents pay the $1,500. It was the first time I realized that if you wanted something and were forced to take action, you could get it.

I often wonder what my life would be like today if my mom had said, "You're right, this is an impossible situation; let's just forget it." Would I have learned to settle for the easiest path? I fear the answer would have been yes. You see, figuring things out, like good posture, is a learned behavior. It's not something you're born with but something you learn. It's a practiced behavior, one that you get better at with time and focused effort. And if you didn't learn it as a child, now is as good a time as any to try. I took my mother's question as a call to action; I was the only person who could realize my goal, and to do that, I needed to get started, and I needed to have faith in myself. Years later I can look back and understand fully how believing in your own potential works. My high school experience was successful and profound for me. It opened new doors and shaped my belief that anything could be flipped. Throughout this book, I will show you, through telling examples and easy-to-follow rules and techniques, how to acquire that ability to flip any situation. But before we begin to work on technique, I'd like to outline more explicitly the principles and benefits of flipping.

THE BENEFITS OF FLIPPING

I can't tell you the number of people I come across on a daily basis in both my professional and personal life who view the world very pessimistically. They can tell you all the things that can go wrong and all the reasons why something won't work before you even get started. They like to think of themselves as practical and smart, but what they have done is build a future of failure. And when things go wrong, as they invariably do, they're never disappointed. The thing they don't consider is what I call the first rule of flipping.

Rule 1: Understand that positive variables are all around.

Understanding that you will never have all the variables under your control means you have to make room for the *unplanned good* as well as unplanned bad. Making room for the unplanned good is expecting uncertainty to turn out with an equal amount of favorability. Let me explain. Typically, when making decisions, people consider and weigh all the things that could go wrong, given a certain set of circumstances. For example, they think the boss will never go for their crazy idea. They can't see the unintended good that may arise from sticking their necks out. Maybe the boss will be impressed by out-of-the-box thinking. Often, we don't have trouble seeing the negative variables and potential loss. Unfortunately, we don't give equal weight to the good and positive. We have been trained by family and society to discount whatever potential good an idea may have if it isn't clearly visible on the surface and its benefit can't immediately be seen. It takes practice to train yourself to consider all the things you cannot see that could go right or better than expected. To start to flip, you need to work on making mental room to account for positive variables that cannot be seen at a given time.

For example, let's go back to my high school experience and take one of the primary obstacles. I had no way to get to and from a school that was more than an hour away from where I lived. My mother did not drive, and my father took the family's only car to work each day—an impossible problem, right? But due to unforeseen good variables, the situation worked out. In fact, that year the town passed a new ordinance allowing students who traveled to private schools to receive free busing. And when the town voted down the provision the following year and all free busing for private school students ceased, more unplanned good allowed me to get to and from school: I had made several friends at school who lived in my area. Since we played sports and had the same irregular travel hours, my friends' parents offered and provided a ride to and from school for me that second year. By my junior year, I had passed my driving test and saved enough money to buy a beat-up old car, so I was able to drive myself.

I would never have been able to account for all these positive variables when making my original decision to attend St. John's. I couldn't see at the time that the town would provide busing or that I would make certain teams or friends. Figuring things out demands that you consider unforeseen good variables. You may be wondering how one can consider all the unforeseen good variables when, in fact, they are *unforeseen*. The answer is simple: *faith*. You have to have faith—a belief in yourself that you will, as my mother said, be "able to figure it out."

The same is true in business. Circumstances and variables change on a daily basis; there are new opportunities arising every minute. You can't move ahead by simply avoiding risk. You have to plan to add some calculated risk to flip your script. Adding calculated risk means that you develop an attitude that allows you to make room for unforeseen positive variables. I've seen it over and over: business executives spend thousands of hours discussing negative risk variables, options, and liabilities, but rarely do they spend time thinking about how business ventures may turn out *better* than expected. At some point you have to realize that you can manage only so much. You must develop faith in yourself that you are doing everything you can to move your business forward and that managed uncertainty will work out in your favor, just as much as it could end unfavorably. Once you develop faith in yourself, things have an incredible way of working out in your favor. Maybe you're thinking that all of this sounds good, but how does one learn to "develop faith"? This leads us to the second rule of flipping.

Rule 2: You need to find faith.

You find faith by letting go of your irrational fears and adding a good variable for every fear, thus giving equal weight to the unforeseen good variables. First, let me say that some fears are good. Rational fears are based on an objective understanding of reality and are normal. I was watching television recently and saw the story of a German woman who clearly could have benefited from some healthy fear. She'd decided to climb over the fence of a polar bear's habitat in her local zoo—during feeding time, no less. It may come as no surprise that she was attacked and bitten by the bear. Thankfully, the brave trainers who worked at the zoo saved her, and she emerged relatively unharmed. Clearly, that woman could have used some rational fear.

Faith will not be able to help you when it comes to rational fears.

Many rational fears are actually good and evolutionarily necessary. It is *irrational* fears that dampen our faith and cause us harm. Irrational fears are not grounded in reality, and an irrational fear ends up being something that can control you. We are full of irrational fears that keep us from having faith. In business irrational fears encompass everything from fear of rejection, fear of authority, and fear of criticism to fear of failure and even fear of success. Such fears keep us from being able to "just figure things out" and making the flip that can propel us in a good direction. Let me tell you a story to illustrate this point.

A good friend of mine, Tom, is one of the most talented sports agents in his business. Hard charging, funny, and smart, Tom has a natural touch with his clients and is on the fast track toward senior management. Unfortunately, Tom suffers from one of the business world's most common irrational fears, a fear of public speaking. On the surface, when you see Tom, this makes no sense. Why would he be afraid to talk in front of a crowd? He's confident, articulate, and successful. But he is deathly afraid of standing alone in front of a crowd and speaking. The interesting thing is that he has no problem contributing as part of a panel or group. It's only speaking solo that causes him to panic. No matter how many times he successfully speaks on a panel, no matter how many times he receives compliments and assurances on his performance, he still remains terrified to speak alone in public. It's an irrational fear that is impacting his business goals, and he'll never be able to find faith and reach his potential unless he can get over it.

Like Tom's, many of our irrational fears are rooted in our upbringing. In his case, success has only fueled his fear because the more successful he has become, the more internal pressure and expectation he has put on himself to always be "on" and to be "perfect." He wants to prove himself worthy of others' admiration. Things really came to a head when Tom received a promotion. That was the good news. The less-than-good news was that senior management wanted him to present at the semiannual corporate meeting. No longer could Tom hide onstage behind a group panel. He was going to have to speak to a group of his peers alone, and he was terrified. He had lost faith. When he thought about his speech, he feared he would lose it all, fall off the pedestal, and everyone would see that he was not perfect, or even as good as they had thought.

We all can feel like Tom sometimes, not wanting to let people down in their expectations of us. But it's those irrational fears that keep us from having faith and being able to "just figure things out." They keep us from making flips and propelling ourselves forward.

Tom called and asked if I would help him prepare for his meeting. I said I would, and we agreed to meet at a local high school auditorium. As expected, with only me sitting in the audience, Tom had no trouble with his presentation. He was funny and on point. I then asked several of our friends, their kids, and their families to come and watch. I also asked my son Hugh's lacrosse team, which had just finished practice, to come and watch. Now, with a semipacked room, it became a different story. Tom's confidence began to slip.

His irrational fear was taking over. He began to feel that everyone was judging him and he wouldn't be able to measure up. He started to sweat and stumble over his words. He needed to get control of the irrational fear. Sometimes it helps to visualize when solving internal issues. In this regard I imagine a balance scale: on one side you have your irrational fears; to gain balance and control, you need to add positive variables to balance out each negative.

To balance his scale, one that was tilting heavily in favor of fear, I gave Tom a positive variable for every negative fear. Tom had three primary negative fears: (1) that people were judging him, (2) that he needed to be perfect, (3) that he would freeze and get stuck. Here's a list of the balancing variables:

1. **Negative fear: Everyone is judging me.**
   Positive variable: People are self-interested.
   People think that when they're speaking in public, the audience is hanging on every word they say. That is just not the case. People are egocentric. Most people are actually thinking primarily about themselves. It's human nature.

What most of the audience is probably thinking about is what they have to do later that day, or else they're checking their BlackBerrys and looking for new emails, wondering what they're going to eat for dinner, or playing back in their minds the fight they had with their partner last night. So, I asked Tom, if you slip up, who cares? Most people won't even remember it. You have to have faith that everyone is really primarily concerned about themselves and their own lives. It can free you from feeling that all their attention is on you.

2. **Negative fear: I need to be perfect.**
    Positive variable: Nothing's perfect; accept it!
    I also advised Tom, whenever he gets nervous, to remember the line "New York would be an incredible place if they just finished building it." Meaning that it's never going to be complete and perfect. Construction will never be completed in New York; the city is a constant work in progress. And so are all of us. We have to develop faith that others will value us as we are. People still love New York with all its noise and mistakes, and you have to have faith in yourself that others will love you and appreciate you even if you make a mistake now and again.

3. **Negative fear: I am afraid I will freeze and get stuck.**
    Positive variable: You can memorize your speech.
    The last piece of advice was purely technical for Tom: when you are nervous about speaking in public, always look toward the back wall; it can't make facial expressions to distract you. I told him that until he was more confident speaking, he shouldn't try to make direct eye contact. I also advised him to memorize the beginning of the speech. It is usually the beginning of anything that is most difficult; if you memorize it and know it cold, you will feel much more comfortable.

The advice helped, and Tom seemed more relaxed on stage. Providing him with concrete positive variables to offset every irrational fear gave him a sense of control over the fears. He counteracted the irrational fear that his speech had to be perfect and Oscar-worthy with the good variable that no one is really so focused on everything a speaker says. He counteracted the fear that all the years of his hard work and success would be in doubt if he made a mistake with the good variable that even if everything went wrong, he was a valuable player in the organization and would still be respected. With those ideas at the front of his mind, he delivered his presentation a week later, to great success.

 Flip Tip: When overcoming irrational fear, balance the scale by adding a positive variable for every negative fear.

Fear is also often a dominating force outside our business lives. Flipping is a great tool that can also be used to take control of fear that afflicts our personal lives. About a year ago, a friend revealed to me that he had been struggling with a secret addiction for years. He had hurt his back some years before, and to alleviate the pain his doctor had prescribed painkillers. Months passed and his back had healed, but he found himself dependent on the drugs to get through his workday. Since his doctor would not write him new prescriptions, my friend was covertly ordering drugs over the Internet. He had managed to conceal his addiction from even his closest friends. Yet as time passed, he started to find that his ability to manage and control his addiction began to slip. He was losing control. He now found himself caught in a tough spot; fear had him firmly in its grip. He was afraid to ask anyone for help; he irrationally felt that even close friends wouldn't understand. He feared that he would be judged harshly for being irresponsible. He feared that his situation was unique to him. He became embarrassed to ask others for help. He lost sleep at night wondering "What if people at work find out?" and "What if my family and friends knew?" Those fears kept him from figuring out ways to resolve his addiction. They were added to an already stressful existence, and ultimately they hurt his ability to experience life to its fullest. He was fear's prisoner, because fear kept him—and keeps us all—from seeing potential positive variables, or from taking necessary action.

One day it became apparent to me that something was desperately wrong with my friend. When I confronted him, he spilled everything: he told me all about his addiction. I was pleased that he had confided in me, and I felt a responsibility to help him release the fear that had taken hold and to help him find faith in himself by seeing the positive variables. But I knew that my telling him not to be afraid probably wasn't going to do much good. Irrational fears don't often respond to good advice. They need to be shown the door. I provided him with the number of a good drug-counseling center—I figured treatment should be left to the professionals—but there were other ways I could help.

A couple of days later, I asked him if he would accompany me on an excursion. We were going to go rock climbing. I'd found a local indoor rock wall and booked a private lesson for the both of us. Neither of us had ever attempted to scale a four-story wall dressed in nothing but a pair of shorts and armed only with what appeared to me to be a thin rope secured to a flimsy harness. When we arrived, we met our instructor, a twenty-something named Abby. She walked us through the fundamentals, which basically included someone climbing and someone she called the "belier," who held the rope in case the person scaling the wall fell.

Abby went on to explain that the trick of a successful climb is reaching up and out for the next hold before you pull yourself up. Once you grab hold of the grip, you need to push your legs upward; however, when doing so, your view is limited. The real issue is the fact that when you reach out you have to commit yourself to that line before you really know if the grip is going to be able to hold you. As you climb higher and the ground below starts looking distant, fear sets in. And when fear sets in, you freeze. You start thinking about all the risks and all the things that can go wrong. You doubt your strength and the ability to hold your weight. When that happens, you're stuck; you're unable to climb higher and unable to get down without falling.

In rock climbing, as in life, there is only one way to go—and that's up. No one runs backward. Our day and the lesson were perfect metaphors for my friend's situation and for many of us stuck in our business and personal lives—a physical manifestation of what he was struggling with internally. To be a successful rock climber and a successful person takes faith. We have to train our rational and irrational minds to work through the fear and learn to take leaps of faith . . . faith that the next hold will propel you upward . . . faith that the person holding the rope will catch you if you fall. Without faith, we'd all be stuck somewhere on the side of our individual mountain, afraid to move forward and unable to get back.

The literal and figurative benefits of the rock-climbing exercise were not lost on my friend. Although I would never want to take even a fraction of the credit for the incredible amount of work my friend has done in turning his life around, he has told me that our day together helped him begin to trust in himself; it was the beginning of, in his words, "a new confidence." It was the perfect choice of words—the root of the word "confidence" comes from the Latin meaning "with faith."

To begin the process of flipping, we first have to be able to recognize that things can and may go better than expected and that if we have faith and can control our fears, we are on the right path. This brings us to the third rule: you have to name your flip.

Rule 3: You have to name your flip.

Sounds easy, right? But is it?

Understanding exactly what it is that we want from our business and our personal lives is often tougher than it seems. It takes honest reflection and soul-searching to figure out what will ultimately give us the most meaning and satisfaction.

At work this is sometimes hard to do, as we are conditioned by the pressure to satisfy external demands rather than internal ones. We push ourselves and our organizations to produce bottom-line results immediately. There can be such a desire to draw within the lines that we convince ourselves that we know exactly what we want. But do we? I am reminded of a breakfast I had with one of my most successful sales managers. A bright, rising star, Ellen had taken the initiative to arrange a breakfast meeting with me to discuss her future. That was not unusual, and I was happy to talk to a valued employee about establishing future career goals.

When Ellen arrived, it was clear that she had rehearsed. During the course of the breakfast she confidently informed me that she was ready and wanted to be groomed for a more senior regional manager role. I quietly listened. She went on to explain all the reasons why she deserved the promotion, including how talented she was and how hard she worked. After she finished, I considered what I knew about her and all that she had just said. She certainly was a major talent, and we would be lucky to have her play a bigger role within the company. But that wasn't my concern. I asked her one question: "Why do you want to be a regional manager?" She looked surprised and said that she had just given me fifteen minutes of reasoning. I listened and replied, "No, don't tell me why you deserve to be a regional manager, because you certainly do; tell me why you want that job."

She stared at me blankly. I explained that I was surprised by her request. Not because I believed she didn't deserve recognition, or couldn't serve the company in an expanded role, but because the woman I knew and worked alongside had previously talked about unhappiness in her personal life. She had expressed her belief that work was all too consuming, that she longed to create balance in her life—to take a cooking class she had promised herself she'd sign up for, among other things. That woman seemed at direct odds with the woman sitting across from me at breakfast seeking a regional manager role, which would require almost constant travel.

As we talked further, it became clear that she didn't truly want the position she was asking for but had convinced herself that it was the only logical next step. She believed that it was her only option, even though the requirements of the job did not match her personal life goals. She had fallen victim, as we all often do, to not understanding the fundamentals of flipping. She was blind to all the positive variables right in front of her: (1) that she was a trusted and valued employee who deserved recognition and (2) that the company should and would be vested in creating new career options for her—options that would eventually meet not only her monetary goals but her life goals as well. She needed to have faith that if she went out on a limb and explained some of her nontraditional ideas for growth together, we would be able to "figure it out."

Ultimately she misfired, because for all that thinking and rehearsing she didn't say what it was that she actually wanted. She didn't want to travel. The problem was that she wasn't sure what she wanted. And she feared that if she did allow herself to say what she really wanted, her desires would not fit neatly into a box and would therefore be dismissed. Knowing what you truly want to flip is essential. How can you create a map if you don't know where you want to go?

Naming your flip is a strictly personal mission. It can't be influenced by what you think you should be doing or by others' expectations. This is the story of your life, and you should never allow anyone else to write its chapters.

Now, I'm not saying that every boss and every person in business and life will bend to your wants and needs just because you can name your desired goal. Naming your flip should be based in a sense of reality. But I can tell you that you will be a heck of a lot closer to getting what you want if you can confidently say what it is that you actually want.

 Flip Tip: To succeed, your goals have to match both your internal and external desires.

HOW TO NAME YOUR FLIP

It may sound overly simple, but to achieve any goal, you have to start with one. Whether it's small or large, all of us have a situation at work or at home that we would like to flip. As I've mentioned before, don't think about all the reasons why something can't happen or all the obstacles in your path. Just think about what it is that you would like to change. Keep in mind that, when flipping, the bigger the challenge, the more work will be required of you. But don't shy away from opportunities because the path seems hard.

Along with this, it's important for you to embrace the notion that you are entitled to dream big. You officially have permission. I often talk to people who lament the situations in their lives, and I can't tell you how many times they don't have an answer when I ask, "What do you want?" It's as if we've all been taught that we have to color within the lines and that happiness and job satisfaction are things made for someone else. To flip, don't worry about the lines.

So how can you learn to dream big? To create a goal, you need to be able to focus on what it is that you really want and edit the selection down to one clear goal, because if you try to do too many things at once, you may not accomplish anything. It's like a person who wants to lose weight, doesn't exercise all year, and then joins a gym. He works out like a fiend the first day, trying to shake off ten years of sedentary behavior in one session, and leaves the gym with his muscles aching. Then he's too sore to exercise the next day and winds up quitting before he even started. To avoid that fate, let's get focused.

As a way of starting to think about what you want and to help focus, consider the following questions: Are you happy at work? Is your career moving in the direction you hoped for? If it isn't, in what direction would you like it to move? Are you interested in a new industry, perhaps? Or what about that promotion you've been looking for? How often do you laugh and when? You could also look at the negative aspects of your personal or professional life and try to get at the root causes, asking questions such as: Do you allow yourself to be taken advantage of over and over again, and why? How will this flip help you achieve your life's mission or purpose? What is the most attractive thing about your goal? Another good question to ask yourself is, if you had a day off and nothing left to be checked off your to-do list, what would you do? What does respect mean to you? And last, what do people expect from you, and what do you expect from yourself? Then ask yourself, how will this goal help you grow in both areas? These questions are intended to get your wheels spinning, opening doors to hidden possibilities.

Whatever the situation, take out a clean piece of paper and write your goals down. Brainstorm, and allow yourself all the mental freedom in the world. What is holding you back? Be realistic and honest. Don't be self-conscious about any of your goals; they are for you and are no one else's business.

Now make a list of ten things that you want in your life, both professionally and personally. You can do it all at once, or you can start it, put the list into a drawer, and come back to it next week. Flipping isn't about who is quickest to completion. This is your movie's happy ending, and it will be done on a timetable you will develop based upon how complex your flip is.

Once you've completed the list of ten things you want, edit and eliminate. Cut out the goals that are less important to you. It's not that you can't go back and revisit them, but think of it this way: you're getting ready for a big night out, and you're standing in front of your open closet. There are many things you could wear, but you can wear only one suit or one dress at a time. All the other choices will have to stay in the closet for another night. Flipping is like that; it will take all of your energy and focus, so you have to narrow your goals down to one. Once you've selected a goal that's a top priority, you can begin the process of flipping.

Over the course of this book, I want to create a framework to help you at every stage. Each step is a necessary part of understanding that in order to rewrite our life stories we need to liberate ourselves from past limitations. After you've winnowed your list down to one top goal, take out a new piece of paper and write it down in big, bold letters. Think about a manageable timetable, and write it down next to the flip. When can this flip be completed effectively? The answers will vary depending on whether your flip is finishing your degree, going back to school for an MBA, getting out of debt, even finding romantic love. Regardless, each flip needs a timetable. Giving yourself a deadline is the best way to ensure that you will take action. Now that you have your goal and a time frame in which to accomplish it, let's get started.

Part One

UNDERSTAND

Life is like an onion:
you peel it off one layer at a time,
and sometimes you weep.

—CARL SANDBURG

Chapter 1

The Power of "So What?"

Life is very interesting if you make mistakes.
—GEORGES CARPENTIER,
TWENTIETH-CENTURY FRENCH BOXER

THERE IS TREMENDOUS VALUE in thinking of alternatives to any situation and creating backup plans. Some of the best advice that I've ever been given—and that works exceptionally well in dealing with both business and personal issues—came from my mother. My mom, who passed away when I was still in my early twenties, was a beautiful and loving woman, but she was also a tough Irish lady, the type who had a cigarette half hanging out of her mouth while she talked on the phone and who treated us like adults even when we were five, as when she'd tell us, "Go make your sandwich for school." She and a generation of women like her managed to walk a fine line between teaching their children love and independence and treating them with a touch of benign neglect. But no matter what, we knew we were loved, and whenever things got tough and people or situations seemed insurmountable or hopeless, my mother would say, "So what?" Asking "So what?" allows you to open windows when you feel as though all the doors are shut. "So what?" pushes you to think against the grain, imagine the worst-case scenario, and then devise new options.

"So what?" can be one of the most unusual and effective personal management tools in your arsenal. It will help you pursue opportunities that may seem out of the norm but that have extraordinary potential, and it will be an important approach for crafting alternative solutions to challenges that arise seemingly out of nowhere. In this chapter, we will discuss how to harness the power of "So what?" to create new ways of thinking, to see hidden opportunities, and to realize possibilities.

The value of "So what?" in business can be critical because too often when we struggle with difficult work and personal situations it is because we are too close to see the issues clearly. If you're honest, you'll admit that when you're personally vested in any situation it becomes much tougher to see new perspectives. When that happens, our perceived options become limited. Think of it this way: when you are too close to have clear perspective, it's the equivalent of looking at Claude Monet's *Water Lilies* in a museum from two inches away. Only when you pull back several feet can you get the full picture. I ask you, are you seeing your circumstances clearly? If you're not, the power of "So what?" will provide some easy techniques that will give you the ability to pull back from any situation where you're too close and gain a new perspective. For example, becoming too close can happen at work when we can become too personally vested in our own ideas or what we think is the "right" outcome that we lose sight of the overall picture. When that occurs, we limit our ability to see other alternatives or connections. Asking "So what?" is freeing; it motivates you to extend beyond what you think of as conventional or comfortable. Practicing "So what?" thinking allows you to take a few steps back from the issue and see it in all its complexity. By saying "So what?" we become unburdened and free from the tyranny of others' expectations and our own adherence to them. So how does it work?

FREE YOUR MIND, AND THE REST MAY FOLLOW

When you say "So what?" to any situation, something instantly happens: you develop a new attitude that breaks you from your expectations and gives you the strength to consider what some might call the "unthinkable"—alternative solutions or paths that take you outside your comfort zone or that force you to redefine the status quo. And that's a good thing. Your mind needs to be free to see previously un-thought-of benefits. "So what?" thinking helps you come up with a Plan B when you need it most. It kicks in when you are hamstrung and feel as though your options for creating new alternatives are limited. This freedom comes from allowing yourself to imagine the worst, then finding the positives in the worst-case scenario and devising new options from there.

There are three important mental advantages that asking yourself "So what?" delivers:

1. It frees your mind from being stuck so that you can see new alternatives.
2. It stimulates fresh thinking and renewed focus.
3. It creates new strategies and contingency plans.

FRANKLY, SCARLETT, YOU'D BETTER GIVE A DAMN

For example, in the publishing world the biggest-revenue issue of the year for fashion magazines is the September issue. September is when fashion and beauty companies launch their new fall ad campaigns. Consumers love that the issues are thick and packed with fresh editorial material and advertising. It is also the issue that has the most financial impact on the bottom line and as a result the most pressure to perform. One year I had a salesperson on my team excitedly tell me several months before the September issue closing that she was going to exceed her revenue number because one advertiser, a fashion company, was planning on running multiple-page ad units in that issue. I said to her, "Sounds good, but what if they don't?" She responded defensively, saying "No, they're going to advertise." It was clear that she was unwilling to consider alternate possibilities. She further explained, "They have to. I need to hit my number, so they're going to." From her response I learned everything I needed to know. The fear of not hitting her revenue number was her real issue and had been combined with the pressure and expectation associated with it. Her fear of failure was strong, and it limited her ability to see alternative viewpoints—and even though she had been told only that the customer was "thinking" of running multiple pages. She was seasoned and should have known that ad campaigns change all the time and it was months before the issue would actually close; in that business anything can happen; it was hardly a done deal. She overlooked all these obvious doubts because blind faith provided the solution to the fear that she might not meet expectations. As a result, she was closed to any alternative views. She had convinced herself that the fashion company advertising was happening. And with that belief, she did not have to further worry about reaching her goals. But was it? Haven't we all felt like Scarlett O'Hara at one time or another when we can't seem to find the answer to a problem or issue and don't want to deal with it? "Oh, I'll think about it tomorrow." The problem is, while you're sleeping tonight, the world and business aren't.

In today's marketplace, asking "So what?" can be useful in creating competitive advantages. "So what?" is a mental tactic that allows you to force yourself to consider alternative viewpoints and plan for the worst. Once you say "So what?" you are free to devise new positive plans and create new outcomes. In that case, I pushed back on her, asking "So what if they don't advertise? What's your plan?" She had none. She had not considered any alternatives. "Look," I said, "I will be thrilled if you are right and everything goes according to your plan, but don't fool yourself: it's gonna be your neck on the line if it doesn't." That dose of reality drew her attention. "Wouldn't you rather try every option?" I pressed. "And in the end, if they advertise and you exceed your budget even further, good for you. But, if you don't use 'So what?' and build for worst case and they change their plans, it'll be too late to do anything and you'll be screwed." I advised her that it was vital to create a backup plan with the time she still had to go out and get some other business. Even though I could see that she understood, she agreed only reluctantly. Why reluctantly?

ASKING "SO WHAT?" MEANS DOING MORE WORK

The reason my colleague was reluctant is simple: we can be reluctant to follow the principles of "So what?" because they almost always require more work. As in the above example, it was easier in the salesperson's mind to assume that the fashion brand's business would be fine and not have to think about it than it was to think and to plan for all the additional hours of work that might be necessary to hit her number if they didn't come through. It's the business equivalent of wanting to lose weight, getting onto a scale, and not wanting to look at the number. Once you see the number on the scale, reality hits you right in the face and you know you're going to have to do some work, and it may be tough. The same is true in business. Asking "So what?" requires that you take action, and taking action means doing more work.

But action also has its rewards, and, as you might have suspected, I chose this example because three weeks after her announcement, the salesperson received the news that the fashion company's inserts were being canceled due to creative reasons. They would be buying a single page rather than the eight pages she had been expecting. It was a big decline in her expected revenue assumptions. The good news was that she had already started to do some additional prospecting. She was working her "So what?" options and plans. She had accepted the possibility that the multipage advertising might not happen. That allowed her to go more aggressively after some accounts that seemed like distant prospects. It worked, and in the end she exceeded her revenue number without their advertising.

How can you be like my colleague and master "So what?" thinking? It takes freedom and focus: freedom to think of new alternatives and focus to carry them out, because freedom without focus won't advance you. But freedom and focus combined can open new, exciting doorways. But how do you develop them?

FINDING FREEDOM MEANS DISRUPTING COMPLACENCY

Luke Williams, a fellow at Frog Design, a global innovation and design firm, is fond of citing Pablo Picasso, who said, "Every child is an artist. The problem is how to remain an artist once he grows up." Williams, the author of *Disrupt: Think the Unthinkable to Spark Innovation in Your Business,* a book about the power of disruptive thinking in marketing, would say that it is impossible to enjoy the freedom and imagination one enjoyed as a child because life "can grind the creativity out of us." So how can one tap into that kind of artistic imaginativeness? What is required is greater freedom and a willingness to be counterintuitive, but in a disciplined way. What I'm saying is, get your head out of the box that it is in and allow yourself to refocus in order to see the possibilities right around you, identify what you're trying to achieve, and then find alternative scenarios for realizing your objective. In Luke's view you can't change the cause of the problem, but to move forward you need to "design yourself a way around the obstacle." Designing your way around obstacles starts with a proper mind-set.

TRY DOING MENTAL PUSH-UPS

Establishing the proper mind-set takes discipline. To create mental space to see alternatives, just as to face looking at the numbers on the scale, you must be mentally available—open and ready to receive information. Think about it, how many times have your family or colleagues tried to talk to you about something, just the basic back-and-forth of life, and you just couldn't focus? Often there's too much clutter in your head. Now imagine trying to deal with larger issues and goals. You need to create mental space, and that takes commitment and a willingness to be open-minded. Think about the clutter in your head like a car's engine. Any mechanic knows that you can't fix an engine while the car is still running. You have to turn it off, take each of the parts out, tinker with them, and then put it all back together. The same is true for creating mental space. You can't get to the bigger goals and issues of your life if your engine is constantly running over all the smaller concerns. And though you can't turn your mind off as you can an engine, you can quiet the noise of the engine in your head.

One of the ways I'd suggest for getting rid of mental clutter and gaining control over the noise is writing down everything in your head on paper. This is a valuable way to prioritize and create mental space. Often, in your head every song is playing at the same volume. To achieve your goals, you have to prioritize them and create an actionable playlist. Once you write them all down on paper, you can see what needs short-term action versus long-term action. This is a technique I use every day; in fact, I demand that all those who work on my teams have a notebook with them at all times and make daily to-do lists. It creates control out of chaos. And once you have control, you have mental space to think about the larger issues and goals that may be holding you back.

 Flip Tip: To create mental space, make a daily to-do list.

ATTITUDE ADJUSTMENT

Now that you've created space to think about your issues, developing an empowering attitude will allow you to see new potential because it will help you close the door on your current method or path, enabling you to create and follow a completely new path. In other words, with a flexible mind-set, you'll be much better equipped to flip the script.

Sticking with what we know or being afraid to suggest an unconventional idea keeps us from moving forward. Asking "So what?" is akin to turning the page. But the question remains, how can you create meaningful action around the idea of "So what?" How can you use this change in attitude to change aspects of your business and personal lives, ultimately leading you to flip the script?

I've divided the approach to using the power of "So what?" into four main sections. But the process doesn't need to be too linear. Please feel comfortable to move back and forth between the steps, depending on your situation. Here's the formula:

1. Think necessity.
2. Identify the worst-case scenario.
3. Mourn the loss.
4. Repackage.

I'll use a real-life example to illustrate exactly how it works, keeping all four factors in mind. I will take you through the steps to show you how you can flip back and forth between steps or repeat certain steps over and over again.

Harnessing the Power of "So What?"

STEP 1: THINK NECESSITY.

The best way to start thinking against the grain and challenging expectations is to organize and prioritize. You need to allow yourself to think of everything that you want to accomplish. I'm not saying you will accomplish everything, but you'll be in a much better place if you do so. Make a list of all your needs. I use the "So what?" approach to start our yearly brand-planning sessions. When I start the meeting, I go around the room and ask each person, "What do you want?" The usual response is a blank look and a "Huh?" And when I say, "No, what is it you want to accomplish? I mean, it could be anything you like." It's constructive, and the beginning of the "So what?" process allows you to think what would be incredible to achieve and then ask what you need to do to get there.

In April 2004 I had some big needs. I was still a relatively young executive, and the magazine I had just been assigned to was stalled in its ability to grow revenue. I endeavored to embark on a major brand-building project. Our goal was to reinvigorate the brand image, increase the magazine's relevancy among young women ages eighteen to thirty-four, and ultimately drive an increase in sales revenues. It was a daunting task for a big and visible business that had lost momentum from a revenue perspective. I had the following needs:

1. I had to create a program or idea that was groundbreaking and original.
2. The idea had to be visible and garner both press and consumer attention.
3. It had to be bold and shake things up, changing consumers' and the industry's perceptions of my brand while staying true to the brand's heritage and core values, which were about empowering women.
4. It needed to demonstrate to my bosses that I could successfully change the course of our business, that I was mature and resourceful enough to reverse the advertising revenue declines.

To begin the challenging process of meeting these demands, I gathered some of my top players and stuck them in a BlackBerry-free room, and together we brainstormed. With each idea we discussed, we would go back to the original list of needs, making sure it met the criteria. If the idea could not meet every objective, we tossed it.

In the end, we came up with the idea of taking our magazine's readers' real stories and converting them into small films. In doing so we would emphasize the empowering nature of our brand. Each of our films would be written by women, star women, and be directed by women, in keeping with the brand's tradition of honoring empowering women and their stories. At the same time, the films were innovative; we'd be delivering the content in a bold, refreshing way. The idea was original; no other magazine had done anything like it before. It was big and new, and it sounded sexy. If done successfully, the films would drive home our editorial difference in the marketplace while aligning us with top celebrities who would give a major boost to the "cool" factor of our brand image.

It was a great idea, but there was one not-so-small problem: neither I nor my right-hand creative director, Leslie Russo, had ever produced a film. We had no idea how to begin the process. And we had no real resources to hire someone who was experienced in the field.

We had clearly identified our needs and come up with a creative solution, but we had some major hurdles to overcome.

 Flip Tip: When you hit an obstacle, ask "So what?" and see what happens.

STEP 2: IDENTIFY THE WORST-CASE SCENARIO.

Once you have identified your needs and have come up with one or many usable ideas, it's time for step 2: identify the worst-case scenario. This is known as *backward induction.* Backward induction is the process of inverse reasoning; that is, working backward from the end of a problem or situation to determine a sequence of optimal actions. It proceeds by first considering the last time a decision might be made and choosing what to do in any situation at that time. This process continues backward until the best action for every possible situation (i.e., for every possible information set) at every point in time has been determined.

It seems complicated, but it isn't. An easier way to look at it is by asking, what are all the things that can go wrong? Then think about what you would do if in fact the worst case occurs. This is your dose of stone-sober reality and a necessary part of harnessing the power of "So what?" Everyone feels better with a plan; facing the realities of what can go wrong can only make you—and your business plan—stronger.

To apply this step to my story, when I began to identify the worst-case scenarios, all the fear that I normally struggle to put out of my mind came rushing in. But as I've learned, in this step it is crucial not to allow fear to take control; you need to control it by creating a reasonable way to manage it. In my case, I considered the following worst-case scenarios:

1. What if the film is poorly produced and I end up being the laughingstock of the industry?
2. These films will be expensive to make; what if I can't get the money or can't get enough money?

3. What if there isn't sufficient good material?
4. What if no one likes the films?
5. What if I fail and I lose my job?
6. What if I can never find another job again?

Taking a leap in a new direction can create a lot of pressure, but it's always worth it if you execute your strategy properly. If our team had been like most in business, we would have thought about the enormity of the many obstacles we faced, both financial and logistical, and might have decided to try something else. But my team was unique. It was a team of "so whatters" who weren't derailed by thoughts of the worst-case outcomes.

STEP 3: MOURN THE LOSS.

The next step in flipping is critical because each of the worst-case scenarios is a scary potential idea squasher. Fear of the unknown can be worse than anything that could occur in reality. Think about when you were a kid; wasn't the fear of what might be hiding in the closet or under the bed always worse in the dark? Don't be afraid, turn on the light! You have the power to do it. It's important to think about all that could go wrong and make peace with it. That's what mourning the loss is—it's coming to terms with the risks involved in creative thinking and putting them into realistic perspective. This allows you to acknowledge that likely some, sometimes many, but rarely all of those worst-case scenarios will happen. Once you've done that, it's time to think about all the unforeseen good variables that could happen, such as, What if the films are successful? What if they really work? What if they lift our brand to new heights? Adding positive variables lightens the risk. By creating a balanced perspective you can now devise some contingency plans, so you are prepared for a managed amount of failure and success.

In the case of my example, once I had put all of the worst-case scenarios on the table and the shock subsided, I realized that an actual loss would never be as bad as what I could imagine. I considered my worst-case scenario, the one where I lose my job and no one would hire me. I was able to put that fear into a rational context. I also countered it with a positive variable: certainly I would be able to find another job. I was talented and hardworking and had built a solid team of players who would follow me. I've found that when put into a rational context, the fear of a loss is often greater than the loss could ever be in reality. This realization can make you feel braver and ready to move on to the next step. When you mourn the loss, you are acknowledging that things will not always go as planned. You have thought about the potential benefits and the potential dangers, and you are ready to accept those risks.

STEP 4: REPACKAGE.

Once you know your needs, have created usable solutions, and have recognized and evaluated the liabilities associated with those solutions, it's time to repackage and ask "So what?" again. So what if I don't know how to make a film and it's a piece of junk in the end? So what? Everyone has to start somewhere. I imagine there was a time when even Steven Spielberg didn't know what he was doing. You need to do this over and over with each possible loss. In so doing you will gain a sense of clarity and strength and begin to see new possibilities and routes. You must identify, mourn, and accept before you can start creating new routes. I think of this step as a mental GPS. For example, when you get into your car, you may have an idea of the route you are going to take to your destination. But as you proceed, the GPS may tell you that traffic in that direction is terrible. What would you do? Most of us wouldn't proceed only to sit in traffic; would you? No, you would look for alternative routes. That is exactly what step 4 helps you accomplish.

Creating new paths or routes is what neuroscientists call "repackaging." In studies that have examined the role the brain plays in effective leadership, the ability to repackage has been found to be essential for accomplishing goals. In his book *Your Brain and Business: The Neuroscience of Great Leaders,* Srini Pillay, an assistant clinical professor of psychology at Harvard Medical School, explains that physical brain activity directly relates to psychological activity.

In fact, it appears that an old dog should be able to learn new tricks. Researchers have concluded that the brain of a sixty-one-year-old is no different from that of a sixteen-year-old in its ability to make new neural connections. So why, as we get older, do we become more resistant to change? It appears that the brain requires some pushing. To repackage and create new pathways or see new options literally means that the brain has to move information from your working memory to the basal ganglia, at the base of your brain. And that takes work and energy.

To understand a little of the science of it, David Rock, the founder of Results Coaching Systems, offers some further information. In an article in the March 2008 issue of *HR Magazine* he says, "Making one decision reduces glucose [blood sugar] levels available for the next decision." That explains why people revert to old habits and the familiar. It just takes less energy. You can literally become exhausted from pushing yourself out of your comfort zone. That is why so many of us are emotionally or psychologically stuck in certain ruts and why we aren't creating new neural pathways. How can you get out of your rut? One of the ways you can overcome the physical aspects of repackaging and train your mind to embrace new solutions is through sleep. It appears that the old saying "Things will look better after a good night's sleep" is actually a great management tool. Evidence suggests that if you go to bed thinking about new routes or possibilities, your mind uses the downtime while you are asleep to move information from your working memory to the basal ganglia. So try making a list of scenarios when you get to step 4, keep them by your bedside, and think about them before you go to sleep. You may wake up with better insights and a refreshed outlook.

FL **Flip Tip:** Go to bed thinking about new ideas or issues you want to solve.

Turning back to my work project, I used the four steps covered in this section over and over again to help our team work through each obstacle and create new solutions to each challenge. Whenever we hit a roadblock and got stuck, we would literally sleep on it and come up with new alternatives in the morning.

A year later we had completed our first short film series, and Leslie and her producing partners had convinced several actresses to donate their time and energy to the project. The films were good, and we were proud of our accomplishment. The first three films centered on the themes of love, friendship, and self-empowerment. Even though they were done on a limited budget, so many people in the entertainment business loved the idea of films made by women for women that as a result many donated their time and talent. The finished products were three incredible little gems.

OPRAH'S CALLING

Then the time came to promote the project. The films, as good as we felt they were, wouldn't matter if no one saw them. And we were terribly afraid that that would be the case, considering that none of the talent had received any money for their participation and were not contractually obligated to promote the films. They were busy celebrities with other obligations; in fact, most had moved on to other projects.

One day I received an unexpected call from the manager of one of the actresses involved in the films, who gave me the good news that she was willing to go on *The Oprah Winfrey Show* to promote the project. Samantha Rosenthal, who manages publicity, and the rest of the team were elated. This was a major win for our brand, and everyone on our team who had worked so hard on the project for a year felt a tremendous sense of pride. There was just one small problem: the manager advised me of the financial requirements needed to win his client's participation in promoting the film, which included the use of a private plane, luxury accommodations, wardrobe allowance, and so on—all of which we had absolutely no budget for. I could feel the sweat drip down my forehead and saw the disappointment in my team's eyes when I told them we wouldn't be able to pull it off. The opportunity had created new and greater expectations, and with them came increased potential losses.

I needed to think about worst-case scenarios and work my way backward. I thought that even without publicity on *The Oprah Winfrey Show*, we'd still be able to call the program a big success. The show would have been icing on an already delicious cake. With that in mind, I felt secure that the world would not end. People often talk about creating organizations in which people can "swing for the fences." This is an all-too-common expression, but I hardly ever see the idea integrated into a real-life business strategy. What business executives need to realize is that their employees can't—and won't— swing for the fences if they're too fearful of striking out and it's their only time at bat. For me, asking "So what?" in that situation helped me take that swing—because I felt confident that we could reach the fences due to the inherent positives I had identified in the project. This attitude and execution can be applied to any situation. Allowing myself to realize how far we'd already climbed up the mountain, not just how much farther we needed to go, had put me on third base already. I didn't need a home run; all I needed was a single, and I could score. I felt free to get back on the phone with the manager and explain that we did not have the funds to make the appearance happen.

Sometimes in your career you are smart, and sometimes you are just lucky. In this case, using the steps of "So what?" put me into a position to take advantage of unforeseen good variables. The situation could have gone either way; uncertainty, I was learning, is a tradition in Hollywood. In the end, the actress believed in the program and was proud of her work—positive variables that we had not originally considered. She agreed to appear and was even generous enough to fly herself and her entourage to the taping at her own expense. We did pick up some incidental costs, but nothing near the original estimate. The basic tenet of the "So what?" approach is to stop hitting your head against the wall by trying to make Plan A work. Plan A may be a great idea, but you need to prepare for Plan B, Plan C, and possibly Plan D. The easiest resolution of my conundrum was to get a budget to pay for the actress. Such thinking is typical of how people tend to go about solving a problem—to remove the primary obstacle. Remember what I said about the pesky boss or irritable mother-in-law?

Sometimes you just can't remove the cause. You need to create new ideas and turn obstacles into usable solutions. Very often those ideas come out of extremely unconventional thought.

Embracing the "So what?" philosophy gives you the mental bandwidth to implement unorthodox methods and entertain eccentric ideas. As a result of our team's first idea to create short films from our magazine readers' real-life stories, the Reel Moments project, as it is now called, has completed seventeen short films. The films are directed by and starring such A-list Hollywood talent as Gwyneth Paltrow, Demi Moore, Kirsten Dunst, Jennifer Aniston, Jessica Biel, and Rosario Dawson, to name just a few. Hundreds of people both in front of and behind the camera have donated their time and talents to making Reel Moments happen over the past six years, including its two incredible producers, Francesca Silvestri and Kevin Chinoy. The project has given seventeen first-time directors the opportunity to expand their creative skills behind the camera and in the process raised thousands of dollars for FilmAid International, a nonprofit organization that uses the power of film to educate and inspire refugees around the world. Not only a commercial success, these films have been critically praised, as well as having been accepted into twenty-six international film festivals, including powerhouses such as Sundance, Toronto, and Berlin over the past five years.

HARNESSING THE POWER OF "SO WHAT?" IN YOUR PERSONAL LIFE

We've seen how using the power of "So what?" can resolve your business problems, but what about in your personal life? Do you feel trapped in your job? You need the insurance or the paycheck, and you can't see any alternatives? Of course there's no time to look for a new job, because very often a job search is a second job in and of itself. When do you say, "Enough, already," assess your goals, determine where you are in achieving them, and, if you're still unsatisfied, look for something new? Earlier in this book I talked about doing some hard work, and facing reality can surely be challenging. You hate to think of yourself as someone who has devoted ten years to a company and is dissatisfied with the results. Yes, you've contributed to the organization, but the corporate world is a political one and perhaps your good work has been outshined by others who are better self-promoters. At what point do you tell yourself that there has to be an alternative? Let's think about the four steps I outlined earlier.

Think necessity: you need your paycheck and your health care insurance, and the 401(k) doesn't hurt. But to fulfill your goals—your other needs—you have to consider alternatives. Maybe, even though you have a paycheck, it doesn't cover your expenses and obligations. Many companies haven't been able to give their employees raises for a year or two, yet expenses from tuition to food, rent, and clothing have increased. In reality it's not really even compensation that drives employee satisfaction. In many top ten surveys on job satisfaction, money rarely ranks in the top five reasons. The most oft-cited reasons are employees feeling overworked and the company's appreciation of an employee's contributions.

In doing this assessment, you might realize that although you are thankful for your full-time job, it isn't setting you up for the future that you desire. So what can you do not only to keep your paycheck but also to enhance your expertise so that you can present yourself as a valuable asset either to your current company or to a new organization?

Let me tell you about a friend of mine who was very well established in her firm. She'd been with a top insurance company for fifteen years or so, ran her own department, and was considered an important asset to the firm. As time went on, the insurance industry changed, and the financial decline impacted her particular area of business; it became more difficult for her to feel fulfilled at work. But the creature comforts of the job—work-at-home days, insurance, lots of vacation time since she'd been there for so long, and the biweekly paycheck—kept her from thinking about alternatives. And although she had money in the bank, she was afraid to touch it for fear of not having it for the proverbial rainy day, particularly since she had three children. She felt stuck but not motivated to make a change.

People may think that if they make no choice, all will stay the same. But they're wrong. Although my friend felt she was unfulfilled and bored, she still felt she was in control. What she didn't think about was the fact that to be successful and productive in your career you need to have a passion for whatever you do. And all her passion was gone. She was just phoning it in. That fact was not overlooked by her bosses. The world does not stop moving because we can't make a decision. If things are not moving forward, then essentially they are moving backward. You need to act, or the world may act for you. And that's exactly what happened. That year she had a less-than-stellar account review. After all her years of service, she had assumed that she had a certain job security. Let me tell you, job security in today's market is a myth, no matter what industry you're in.

Now, after fifteen years of work, she had to face the harsh reality that her job was in jeopardy. It was just the jolt she needed. After long and deliberate consideration, thinking about her family needs, what her future might look like, and how to juggle her family's financial obligations with the long-term goals she had for herself, she decided to make a bold move and leave her job and enter law school. The rainy day had arrived, and she was brave enough to face it. The first year of juggling family and the demands of full-time law school were tough on both her and her family. Initially she was concerned that she had traded in one stressful situation for another. Her husband complained that she was never around, her children complained that she was always late. And she had her own doubts as she struggled to stay awake at night studying while she could hear her family laughing and watching *American Idol* in the room next door. Success takes hard work; there is no magic pill to flipping the script. It takes commitment and determination. But in the end the hard work is worth it. In 2011 my friend made partner in her law firm.

The point of this story is to emphasize that you cannot let fear—whether conscious or unconscious—keep you from exploring new opportunities. Be unafraid to say "So what?" and map out a future in which you can accomplish all the things you dream about. Be honest with yourself about where you are in your situation; identify what you absolutely need to happen to implement the changes you want to see. The critical thing is to be unafraid to stare your future, whether immediate or long term, in the face and ask yourself whether or not your current path will lead you to success. If the answer is no, then say "So what?" and figure out what you need to do to make things happen.

As you develop the ability to see what doesn't work and the creative ability that comes with saying "So what?," I want to be sure that you are also comfortable with the idea of being successful. The first thing to do is believe that success is how you define it. You don't need anyone's permission to improve your situation. In the next chapter, you'll learn why it's so important to accept the gifts that life provides and how to turn them into a means for achieving your goals. Every person has been given gifts and innate talents. The trouble is that sometimes we don't see them clearly or know how to harness their power. Like Dorothy with her ruby slippers in *The Wizard of Oz,* each one of you has everything you need already inside of you to achieve your goals.

Chapter 2

Ruby Slippers

You've always had the power.

—GLINDA, THE GOOD WITCH,
IN *THE WIZARD OF OZ*

IF IT'S UP TO each of us to improve our situation, how and where can we get started? The answer may be staring at you from the television screen. One of my favorite films while growing up was *The Wizard of Oz,* an endearing children's classic that can provide an appropriate metaphor for many of the opportunities and challenges we face in business today. This chapter is called "Ruby Slippers" because it is important for each of us to know that, like Dorothy, we already have the power to change our lives and circumstances.

Opportunities and challenges are wonderful gifts. Believing that you are worthy of challenges and deserving of opportunities, however, is a learned behavior. A few years ago, I attended an event at which the tennis phenomenon Billie Jean King was being honored. She was more than just a star athlete, she was an incredible speaker and motivator. I remember being moved several times during her speech, especially when she explained her unique philosophy of life, upon which she later based a best-selling book, *Pressure Is a Privilege.* Her premise was simple: pressure is a privilege that we all need to take advantage of.

King believes that you're lucky if you have pressure in your life and that instead of feeling crushed by it, you should learn to see it as a benefit and use it as a motivator. In her eyes, when there are high expectations of you, you will rise to the occasion and achieve great things. Furthermore, she says, once you attain a certain level of success, people will continue to expect success from you. Pressure, then, as a part of this cycle of success, plays an important role in how we value ourselves. She feels that you are lucky if others want something from you, because that means you have achieved something of value, something worth wanting.

In the preface to *Pressure Is a Privilege,* the actress Holly Hunter wrote about her many visits with the tennis legend as she prepared to portray King in the made-for-TV movie *When Billie Beat Bobby.* The actress noted what an incredible person King was because she took it as her responsibility to break down barriers and inspire others. "Billie Jean King," she enthused, "is a global treasure. Few born leaders truly have the courage and stamina to live up to responsibilities that come with the gifts they have been given."

Though King shouldered this responsibility admirably, understanding and valuing our individual gifts isn't always easy. But we should acknowledge that each of us has them. Do you know what your gifts are? Are they the same gifts that others tell you you have? In this chapter we will explore how to acquire the personal and professional poise, discipline, accountability, and moral character necessary to appreciate your gifts and learn how to use them to realize your flips.

In juggling our busy, overscheduled personal and work lives, although we might be able to appreciate that pressure is a privilege, more often the pressure we experience can seem like a terrible weight rather than a motivator. It takes a different kind of attitude to turn challenges into means of achieving goals. A little later in this chapter I'll present some tools and strategies you can use to develop the type of mental toughness that Billie Jean King and other world-class athletes possess and that can work wonders off the court, too. Those skills will help you propel yourself forward in pursuit of your goal. But before we can talk about others expecting success from us, we have to learn to expect success from ourselves. Self-confidence will equip you with the ability to handle any pressures or challenges you might face when flipping your script.

SUCCESS STARTS WITH ME

Understanding that we should and can fix our own problems and our own lives is essential. Only you can define what success is to you. And you need to do it on your own terms. Too often we can feel burdened by all of the expectations that others put on us or become paralyzed by the fear that we may not have the skills or ability to effect positive changes in our lives. But there are ways to put this fear and self-doubt out of our minds and harness our innate talents to live up to the high expectations we should all have for ourselves.

A few months ago, I took my ten-year-old daughter, Helena, horseback riding for the first time. She said she was excited, but when we arrived at the stable and she got onto a horse, she started to cry. It had looked a lot easier when she was standing next to the horse than when she was sitting on top of it. I was worried that she would quit because she was afraid and didn't believe she could do it. This attitude is similar to many work situations and people I encounter daily, individuals who would rather quit and not even try than risk failure. They don't want to take on the personal risk and accountability that must accompany recognition and advancement. This lack of responsibility can be deadly for business; too often executives stay safely on the ground, in their own comfort zones, afraid to make decisions or risk change, and their businesses suffer as a result. Flipping takes self-confidence and an understanding that you are personally responsible for your successes and failures. It's about turning that understanding into a way of driving forward. How can you try something new and benefit from the experience if you are too afraid to let go of your fears?

Fear paralyzes, and it isn't picky: children, adults, politicians, and even those you assume are incredibly successful have all been affected by it. I can't tell you the number of times I've been in meetings in which senior-level players weren't honest and direct about what they thought, even though they had the right answers. They kept quiet for fear of hurting someone else's ego or embarrassing themselves. Dealing with pressure, expectations, the fear of being wrong, and standing up to the boss are all necessary if you want to change your life for the better. You may ask, "Where can I find the courage, skill, and discipline to handle pressure?" My philosophy is that, like Dorothy in *The Wizard of Oz,* most of us already have everything—the skills and the courage—we need to flip our personal scripts and get what we want.

As you may recall, at the beginning of *The Wizard of Oz,* Dorothy is searching for something, an adventure she feels is missing in her life. After a twister hits her home, she finds herself in a strange land, where she makes several friends who also feel that they are lacking something: a heart, brains, courage. None of them feels capable of achieving his goals on his own, so the group sets out in search of a wizard who will give them what they believe they need. When Dorothy and her friends get to Oz near the end of the film, they discover that the wizard is a fake and therefore can't help them. But after that devastating realization, they are awakened to the incredible knowledge that the power to grant all of their wishes was theirs the entire time. Dorothy's wish was to go home, and she put herself into many compromising situations throughout the film because she didn't realize that all she needed to do was click her ruby slippers three times and she would be sent back into the loving arms of her family. She should have had faith that she had the ability all along, and so should you in overcoming your challenges.

Like Dorothy, in business and in life we need to understand that there is no wizard and there are no magical powers that make someone else more successful than you. The power to grant our own wishes is inside each of us. We just have to learn to be comfortable being our own fairy godmother. Like Dorothy, who sought the wizard, we may feel that we need outside permission or validation to be able to ask for or accomplish the things we want in our lives. That just isn't the case; all you really need is patience, a belief in your own abilities, and a measurable action plan. But why don't we do it?

 Flip Tip: You have the power to improve your life today.

CONFIDENCE IS CONTAGIOUS

The answer to the question of why we don't just make it happen became evident recently when I was casting for a host of a new food-based reality television series we were developing. We looked at more than thirty chefs who were extremely likable and had the necessary cooking expertise. The issue wasn't finding people who were qualified and attractive; it was finding people who believed they could do it. All of the candidates were ambitious and interested in expanding their names and careers; in fact, many of them had done television before. But it was just incredible the number of times even the most outwardly skilled chefs sought validation and approval. The key to changing your life starts with self-confidence, and self-confidence is contagious. In the end the chef we hired actually had the least experience; in fact, he had never been on camera before, but when he walked in the door, he commanded the most attention. What he did have was the greatest self-confidence. He convinced the group that he was born to do the show. And it worked. Think about it: how can you convince others of your talents if you yourself are not convinced?

There is a tremendous power in understanding what skills or talents you already have and helping others to see them clearly. A great example of believing in your own talents and skills is someone I've met through business, Andy Cohen, the executive vice president of original programming and development at Bravo. He transformed himself and his career, making the challenging transition from working behind the camera to starring center stage. To get others to see you in a different light takes self-confidence and tenacity, and Andy has both in spades. As reported by Emma Rosenblum for a January 2010 article in *New York* magazine, the story goes that while Andy was working behind the scenes developing programming at various television networks, his original dream was to be on-air talent rather than a behind-the-scenes programmer. Many of us, when we start our career, take the path of least resistance to avoid hardships. The problem is that sometimes, not realizing the consequences of that choice, we find ourselves in our careers, ten years later, not in the place we wanted to be. Andy says, "I was like, 'Screw this, I'm not moving to the middle of nowhere to be a reporter when I could have this cool life behind the scenes in New York.'" So he worked for years behind the scenes in television production. But he also had a flip that would not go away, even as he achieved great success behind the cameras: he felt he also had something to offer in front of them. All he needed was the confidence to go after his dream job. The truth is, it's never too late to flip the script. Cohen never gave up on his ambition to get in front of the camera, and he did it! Cohen's TV appearances grew out of emails he sent to Bravo president Lauren Zalaznick in 2007. "I was sending dishy reports from the set of a show, and she was like, 'You have to start blogging for us.'" So he did. Then Cohen started getting more gigs, and the network saw his obvious talent; one small goal led to another, then another.

Now, five years later and the host of his own highly successful show, *Watch What Happens Live,* on Bravo, Cohen can attribute his success to self-belief. He has had a head-on collision with destiny. "I don't have a lot of self-doubt or cracks in my self-confidence," he admits, "but putting yourself out there every week and throwing your opinions around on TV would cause you to maybe go home and say, 'Who the hell am I to say anything?'" To that I say, Why not you, Andy?

Though Andy's story is inspiring, you may be asking, how do I take the first step? The answer is simple: until you test the limits and push yourself, you'll never know how far you can go. Keep that in mind as you read this chapter. You should constantly be testing yourself. Ask yourself honestly, have you pushed your talents to the limit? Are you too comfortable to change? Have you stuck your neck out and tried something new? Some of the questions you can ask yourself if you are truly pushing your limits are:

1. When in your career were you most terrified? What happened?
2. Are you terrified now?
3. When in your career were you most engaged? What happened?

4. Are you most engaged now?

5 What is most important to you, ranked in order: money, power, or fame?

6. What are you willing to give up and sacrifice to achieve money, power, or fame?

If the answers to these questions are that you are more comfortable than terrified, less engaged than you once were, and not willing to give up much for money, power, or fame, it's time to start pushing yourself to new limits. The process starts with taking personal responsibility.

 Flip Tip: Until you test your limits you have no idea how far you can go—so push.

TAKING RESPONSIBILITY

Before we can understand the power of our own ruby slippers, we have to understand that we got ourselves to wherever it is that we are. Just as there's no wizard who can make everything right for us, there is no demon that has made everything wrong. It's just us. If you're reading this book, I'll assume that you're doing so because you have something in your life you want to change—a script you want to flip. A critical step in beginning the process of changing anything is admitting that each of us is responsible for his or her choices and the consequences of those choices. Facing this reality can be difficult. It feels much better to pass on the responsibility, either directly or indirectly, to someone, anyone. But in order to win, we first need to accept the challenge of accepting that we—and not anyone else—are in control of our destiny.

People sometimes curse fate and ask, "Why me?" That assumes that the world is revolving around you and there is someone else who is punishing you. To that I say, Why not you? No one gets through this life without some struggles. We have to begin, like Billie Jean King, to see those struggles as teaching moments and opportunities to push ourselves to new heights.

There is the incredible healing power of taking personal responsibility. It can feel like lifting a weight off our backs that we have been carrying for years. Starting the process of personal accountability takes honesty. There are some questions we need to ask ourselves to be able to accept and use this honesty. Ask yourself the following:

1. What can I do *right now* to fix the situation I want to change? It can be a big or small action, but it has to be something.
2. What did I do that contributed to getting me where I am?
3. What could I have done differently?

Like Dorothy and the ruby slippers, we have within us the power to get to where we want to go. The journey to accountability is about finding the origins of our behavior, and it begins with taking personal responsibility.

This is a very tough process. Some of the techniques I've found helpful on my journey in understanding accountability came from noted expert and speaker John Miller. In his book *QBQ! The Question Behind the Question,* which is devoted to the practice of personal accountability, Miller mirrors my view, saying "Personal accountability is about each of us holding ourselves accountable for our own thinking and behaviors and the results they produce." The main idea driving Miller's book and the techniques he offers is that buried under any question you are asking yourself is another question that gets to the heart of the matter. For example, let's consider questions I hear all the time, such as "Why can't my boss see that I'm totally promotable?" and "Why don't my account prospects ever call me back?" The QBQ way is to express those concerns differently and home in on what the person asking the question is doing or not doing. If you want to get to the heart of the problem, ask yourself, "What did I do that may have caused this?" Miller's approach is to ask only questions that begin with "What" and "How." It clears the way to getting to the real issue. Another way to look at the question "Why can't my boss see that I'm totally promotable?" would be "How can I get my boss to see that I'm promotable?"

The second approach is to change the subject to "I," not "they," "he," "she," and so on. This change puts you right in the center of the challenge. For example, ask yourself, "What can I do to get this business prospect moving closer to our doing business together?" rather than "Why don't *they* email or call me back when I call?"

When you look at yourself in this context, you get the power I talked about earlier. You're empowered because now you can flip a situation. You can take action. I always tell my teams that you can either curse the darkness or turn on a light. Thinking about problem solving in this way, you can probably identify a lot of things you can do differently. How about you fly out and meet your business partners and offer to discuss their contract concerns in person? What if you were to endorse one of their current product lines or support it in some way? A great example of this was a large nail polish manufacturer with which my company had done business for many years. But lately we'd struggled to grow the business. At the time of that crisis, I was not taking personal accountability. I was frustrated and spent my time thinking "Why don't they ever increase their business?" I figured we had been working hard to service the account and its business with us was not growing, even though it had grown with some of our competitors. I blamed the client, thinking "Why won't *they* throw us a bone?" Then I decided I had to change the way I was thinking about the situation; I needed to take on some accountability. So I changed the way I phrased the question in my head from "them" to "me." I asked myself, "What have *I* done to grow our business with them? What new ideas or retail programs have *I* brought them to extend our relationship and increase our revenue?" The answers were simple: nothing and none. So how could I be surprised that our business with the client wasn't growing? With that realization, *I* reenergized my efforts, creating fresh ideas and taking action. As a result, within two years our business with the client nearly doubled. Accountability starts with asking the right questions, but it needs to be followed by taking the right actions.

Once you've identified your role in any situation, you need to back it up with action. I often ask my teams, "How do you eat an elephant?" The answer is "Bite by bite." The same is true for taking action: start small, perhaps by being accountable for less arduous goals. What if you were to consistently beat your deadlines by at least one day? Colleagues wouldn't have to hound you for a missing report or business plan, the boss would see that you are on top of your work and likely ready for more responsibility, and you'd prove to yourself that you are in control. Then you could take it from there, adding more challenges to your list incrementally. Those victories would help you build the confidence you'll need as you tackle the more difficult goals ahead. But as we all know, this process is not easy and there are many roadblocks that can arise in our quest for accountability; the most significant of these is the tendency we all have to blame each other.

BLAMESTORMING

Over the years I've worked with many new executives coming up the ranks, and accountability has continuously proven to be one of the hardest lessons to learn at any age. It's difficult because people in business are often most concerned with being right, placing blame, and avoiding the wrath of their bosses, customers, or clients. I've often joked that instead of the all-too-popular term "brainstorming," most client meetings I've been in tend to be more like "blamestorming," with no one taking responsibility for decisions or choices made. To see if you're guilty of blamestorming, ask yourself these four questions:

1. Do I blame others? Colleagues, clients, or family members? (E.g., "He never told me it was due today.")
2. Do I make excuses to avoid responsibility? (E.g., "I couldn't get to that email because I was traveling.")

3. Do I ever apologize?
4. Do I complain rather than try to make a situation better?
   (E.g., "They really need to fix that.")

If you answered yes to any of these questions, you have some room to grow. Many of us are guilty of making mental note of all those who have wronged us in business or life and who we believe are responsible for all that is not right with our circumstances. Blaming others is a beast that will never be satisfied, and this behavior can derail your career goals. A recent example of this occurred with a friend of mine. At her company, one of the sales executives was on the warpath. He was upset because he had recently lost a major piece of business to a competitor, and neither the client nor its agency had ever given him a rationale for why they had pulled the business. He felt he had serviced the account well and had good relationships. Now that the business was gone and he was receiving no explanation or response to his calls, he was upset. To vent his frustrations, he decided to send the client a pointed email inquiring why it had pulled the business. As he wrote and then rewrote the email, he was aware that his tone was a bit aggressive and might have bordered on unprofessional. He knew enough to stop and think about the email's tone, and with that in mind he looked for a second opinion. He forwarded the email to his ad manager to review. But the manager was busy and didn't read the lengthy email thoroughly, so when the manager was caught running down the hall by the impatient salesperson looking for feedback on whether to send the email, the manager said, "Go for it."

One tap of a finger, and the email was sent. Two days later, all hell broke loose. Not only had the email been sent to the beauty company's advertising agency, but the salesperson had also copied the retired company patriarch. Having been unaware of the situation, my friend, the manager fumbled to reply when she received an angry call directly from the president of the ad agency. She apologized profusely, then told him she would find out what had gone on and get back to him in a day.

The next thing she did was call in the salesperson and ask him to explain what had occurred. The first thing the salesperson said, instead of "I'm sorry, that was a bad idea," was "I ran it by my ad manager for approval, and he said 'Go for it.'"And so the blamestorming began. When the president of the agency called the ad manager into his office and inquired why he had approved the email, the manager's response only continued the chain. His excuse was "I was so busy working on trying to get out another project that I told him, 'I trust you, just go with it.'" The "I trust you" part clearly put the blame back onto the salesperson.

Unfortunately, this type of behavior takes place in business every day. My friend was disappointed that neither one had taken any responsibility, both had made excuses, and neither had apologized at first. This lack of accountability isn't only bad for businesses, it's bad for your career. Not only had it weakened my friend's view of his employees' business acumen and maturity, it had also potentially damaged the relationship between manager and salesperson, not to mention the havoc it wreaked on the company's relationship with the client. The situation left the salesperson feeling as though his manager did not have his back when things went south and the manager feeling as though the salesperson had thrown him under a bus. When people blamestorm, nobody wins.

As a result of the email, both the manager and the salesperson wrote letters of apology to the client and the agency. And when it was time to recommend the manager for a promotion, his behavior had lasting consequence; my friend could not in good conscience give him a positive recommendation.

THE PLAYGROUND STORY

Whenever my team members come to me and place blame on a client, their teammates, or bosses, I remind them that they have a choice: do they want to be right, or do they want to reach a positive outcome? I generally tell a story that's not work-related to illustrate this point. It's a story about a kid in the fifth grade.

A young boy had become the target of two playground jerks who

picked on him every day. After a week or two of bullying, the kid finally went home and told his mother. Instead of saying, "Poor you,"
she asked a simple question: "What do you think you could have done
to bother them?" "Bother *them*?" he thought indignantly. "I'm the
victim. I wasn't bothering them. You should be trying to help *me*."

Of course, no one wants to hear that he might somehow be at
fault, particularly in a situation where he appears to be the wronged
party. I'm sure that some of you who are reading this may be annoyed because it seems as though I am justifying the bullies' behavior
and blaming the victim—which I am not. Bullying is wrong. It is
never acceptable. But that type of thinking is about wanting to be
right rather than accepting responsibility and moving forward. Ultimately, regardless of whether you believe you've been wronged, you
have to ask, "What is it that I want? Do I want to be victimized,
requiring others to come to the rescue, or do I want the bullying to
stop and move on?" It's the difference of asking "What?" as opposed
to "Why?"

Getting back to our fifth grader, after thinking about it, he returned to school and, rather than seeking outside help, as in *The Wizard of Oz,* trying to turn others against the two bullies, or even telling
his teachers, he thought about what role he might have played in the
situation. He quickly realized that the year before he hadn't invited
either of the kids to his birthday pool party. He wondered if that
was the seed that had grown into their dislike of him and ultimately
the teasing. Understanding that his actions might have played a role
in their behavior was just the opposite of taking the blame; it was
liberating. As a result of that realization, he devised a plan to fix the
situation.

The next day, he invited the boys over to his house after school.
Though one of the boys did not show up, the other did. That was
enough to break up their united front, and it stopped the bullying.
In fact, the two boys had fun playing that day. They even became
friends—such good friends that, as the years passed, the former
schoolyard bully ended up standing up in front of friends and family

as a groomsman at his friend's wedding. Life has an interesting way of working out once you stop blaming and start accepting responsibility. It can be liberating because it's about acknowledging that we determine how we think and feel. Our positive or negative reactions have a ripple effect both personally and in our careers. Unfortunately, in my own career I had to learn that lesson the hard way.

RETURN TO SENDER

As the thirty-one-year-old new magazine publisher, I experienced directly how damaging denying responsibility can be—and the lasting impact it can have on one's career. My business, like most today, can be highly competitive, but sometimes competition can be used as an excuse for bad behavior. It was the first time I was leading an entire organization. And people looked to me to set the tone. The magazine I was working for at the time was in an upswing in terms of sales and circulation. That did not go unnoticed by our direct competitors, who were fearful of our success. I had been told several stories, which I believed, about one competitor who was out in the market telling our best clients that we were financially unstable and would be going out of business soon.

Instead of being mature and confronting the person directly, accepting that our success would and should make the old guard nervous, or even trusting that our clients wouldn't believe the gossip, I indulged my ego based on what I believed was unjust treatment. I wrapped myself in victimhood and righteousness. That allowed me to believe that anything I did in response was warranted. Competition in business is good, right? Wasn't that what had made me successful? So, to counteract the negative press I felt we'd been given, I did my own negative mailing. I sent an unmarked negative article that had been published in the paper, criticizing my competitor, to all the competitor's clients. It was sent in a simple white envelope with no logo or return address. It was the wrong thing to do. I was young and felt so righteous; I believed that one supposed bad deed deserved another and that the competitor deserved some negative attention for all it had said about our brand. I didn't take any personal responsibility; I was blaming someone else for my actions. I didn't believe that I was accountable for my behavior.

As you might imagine, this story didn't end well. The competitor traced the postage code to our mail office, and its president called our president to criticize my actions harshly. At the time I pointed the finger of blame, saying "But he did this, and he did that." With my defenses up, I was blind to the fact that no one had forced me to send the letter. But because I didn't want to admit wrongdoing, the career that I had worked so hard for was at risk, and the team that looked to me for guidance and mentorship was fearful and disappointed. I had implicated the entire organization. Now both my team and I were in jeopardy.

Standing up for the choices you make is an essential part of claiming accountability and responsibility. Whether it's something you did, didn't do, or did wrong, you need to own up to the behavior and use it as a catalyst for improvement. People sometimes talk about "Aha!" moments. Well, mine happened right then and there in my boss's office. It was as if a lightbulb went off over my head. I realized that no matter what I thought others had done to me, I still had to look at myself in the mirror in the morning, and I was the one who had to like and respect the guy looking back at me. I decided at that moment to grow up and stop making excuses. I told my boss that the competitors were right and that I deserved whatever career repercussions were coming my way. She said she was not certain what would happen and would get back to me. I apologized and left her office. The next morning I called my competitor and asked if I could come in, as I wanted to apologize to him and his editor in person. He agreed. When I was finished, I felt as though a weight had been lifted off me; it felt good to accept responsibility. It was not a calculated move, and they were clearly angry. But when the dust settled, I kept my job, and I worked hard for years to repair the damage I had done to my reputation. Today, when people ask me what is one of the greatest predictors of business leadership, I say accountability.

Ask yourself, Does your behavior show a lack of integrity? Do you fail to honor your commitments? Do you blame others for your choices or your circumstances?

If you answered yes to any of these questions, you've got some work to do. If you want to figure out how to change your behavior and win, keep reading.

THE RIGHT STUFF

Throughout this chapter, I've talked about personal responsibility. Integrity and moral character are traits that are sometimes hard to come by. Certainly, when we have a knee-jerk reaction to a contentious situation or a threat, high morals can fly out the window. It's easy to say you want to do what's right, but what can you rely on to ensure that you'll do the right thing?

What does it take to change your behavior—your actions and your words—so that you own the choices you make? Albert Einstein said that the definition of insanity is doing the same thing over and over and expecting different results. So if what you've been doing isn't working, it's time to try some new ideas. Business has never been in greater need of individuals who represent the best in all of us. When people treat others and themselves with respect, they tend to interact better socially, have more and longer-lasting friendships, and recover from traumatic situations faster and with less lasting impact. If you are ready to up your game on the accountability front and you're not certain of the right thing to do, try asking yourself:

WHAT WOULD SUPERMAN DO?

Whenever you are in a moral dilemma and you're not certain what the right move is, ask yourself what Superman would do. It may sound childish, but think about it. If you were to go to any movie theater over the past decade, you would have seen superheroes and heroines fighting for what's right on the silver screen. I would argue that such films set box-office records because we all have an innate desire to see someone who is incorruptible, who will always do the right thing. We want the same thing in business today. Companies want to work with and promote individuals who know what the right thing is and how to bring it about. Can you imagine Superman blaming his coworkers or complaining?

Without a positive outlook and confidence in your ability, you can't flip the script. Once you have those things, you need to accept the fact that you are in control of your actions and decisions and that you have the capabilities needed to make good decisions. Think with the end result in mind, and behave accordingly. You can succeed, you can win, and you can do so with integrity. Once you have integrity, you will begin to see more clearly that your actions may be contributing to self-sabotage and derailing your personal or professional life.

Chapter 3

"The Boss Hates Me" and Other Acts of Self-Sabotage

When a man points a finger at someone else, he should
remember that three of his fingers are pointing at himself.

—ANONYMOUS

ONE OF MY FAVORITE action-movie franchises has always been the
James Bond series. Each high-adventure film features a villainous
character who is attempting some form of global sabotage. Though
Bond always fights those outside evils handily, one wonders if he'd be
as successful if the sabotage had come from within. In chapter 1 we
worked on opening ourselves to possibilities by asking the powerful
question "So what?" Then, in chapter 2, we challenged our personal
expectations of success to create a philosophy of personal accountability. In this chapter I want to dig deeper into understanding our
own psychology and the psychology of others, shed light on how we
can sometimes become our own worst enemies, and offer some techniques to flip the script on our shortcomings in order to create advantages and win the support of others.

Accomplishing your goals takes a lot of mental preparation.
There are many aspects of ourselves that if left to their own would
sabotage every effort we make to become fulfilled and successful.
Unhealthy patterns of behavior or negative personal interactions
can make perfect sense to the protagonist, even though they may be
perfectly senseless. No one is immune to this behavior. It's when you

realize that such acts of self-sabotage may be limiting your career prospects that you need to change.

NOT SO NEUTRAL IN SWITZERLAND

I remember one time when I could have used my own advice. When I was younger, I had a much harder time listening to people. I was often my own worst enemy because I was well on my way to becoming one of those people who thought he was always right. Talk about a career killer! This self-determined expertise extended to areas where I had direct knowledge, but shamefully it was not limited to those. I remember one time in particular when having read this book would have come in handy—that and a major do-over would have been ideal.

The incident took place several years ago, when a group of colleagues and I traveled for the first time to what would become our yearly pilgrimage to the World Watch and Jewellery Show. This is a very upscale convention where the world's top brands of watches showcase all of their new products. It takes place each spring in Basel, Switzerland. If you know anything about the Swiss, you know that they like their watches and they like their protocol. Everything in the country runs with exacting and sometimes uncompromising precision. Let me remind you, it was my first time in the country. Even though I knew nothing of Swiss business customs, I was one of those "uncoachable" people who just couldn't be told anything. I wasn't open to listening. And although one of my colleagues, Pam, had lived in Switzerland for an extended period, I didn't really want to hear what she had to say about the subject of Swiss business protocol. I knew everything—or so I thought.

During the third day of the trip we had a 10 A.M. appointment to meet with a marketing director from an upscale watch brand to see its new line of watches. Before the meeting, our team—three editors and two advertising execs (myself and Pam)—met for coffee to discuss our strategy. Whereas the editors' goal at the show was to see all the new watches for future editorial content in the magazine, Pam and I were really the unwanted guests, there to try to secure advertising; we were essentially using the meeting with editors to gain direct access to the client. It's important to note that although we were colleagues, Pam and I were extremely competitive.

In our strategy discussion, Pam tried to explain how she thought we should tackle the meeting, given her past experience in the country, but I wouldn't have it. I was going to be in control. I wanted to be the leader. She suggested a soft approach. She explained, "The Swiss can be tricky. It would take tact on our part not to overstep the company's excitement about their new watch product with our advertising discussions of business. In my experience, in Switzerland more than in the U.S., politeness is valued."

"Come on," I said, "business is business anywhere." With that we headed out for our appointment. I remember Pam rolling her eyes at my arrogance. When we reached our appointment, we were greeted by an attractive middle-aged Swiss woman of Japanese descent; on the left-hand pocket of her suit she wore a name tag that read "Suga Lynn." She was reserved, and her English was good but not excellent. I extended my hand and said, "Hello, Suga, I'm Bill Wackermann, and we are so excited to see what your new watches look like." I then took control of the meeting and introduced our editors: "Suga, this is Hyla, Mark, and Patrick." Suga smiled awkwardly and started to walk us through the six new watches, each beautifully encased in glass in a large wooden standing display. With the editors busy scribbling notes, each time she pointed out some new watch innovation or feature and before Pam could speak, I was quick with a comment and an approving nod. "Yes, Suga, I like that." "Wonderful, Suga, how much will that retail for in the States?" Despite the fact that Suga's look suggested a bit of annoyance, which I chalked up to Swiss formality, I continued. In my head I thought I was showing Pam that business was business anywhere and I didn't need to listen to her advice.

As we finished the preview of watches, I was ready to strike. It was time to talk about our magazine as a potential ad vehicle. I asked, "Are you planning on advertising this, Suga?" Suga was a bit cold, but I was just getting warmed up. I was not going to pay attention to her chilliness—so I went for it. Just before I started on my ad pitch, a man approached us. From what I knew of the account, he was the worldwide marketing director and Suga's likely boss. "Sorry to interrupt," he said. "No worries," I cut him off. It suddenly occurred to me that whatever Suga's issue was, I could win her back to my side by showing her my professional generosity. "No worries at all," I continued with a broadening smile on my face. "Suga did an excellent job." He looked puzzled, and he spoke curtly. "Okay, then," he said with his heavy German accent. "Glad to hear." He went on, "Lynn, can you come talk to me when you're finished here?" "Yes, certainly," she responded.

Lynn? Who was Lynn? I looked over my shoulder to see the smile on Pam's face widen. "Will you please excuse me?" the former Suga, now Lynn, asked. "Yes, just one question," one of the editors replied. As Lynn moved to finish up with the editor, Pam moved closer, and her grin became unbearable. She could barely contain her glee as she said, "In Switzerland, they sometimes put the last name first on the name tags. Nice work, Wackermann Bill." Ugh.

Your takeaway here is to remember that although you can't always change who you are or your natural tendencies, you need to do so in some cases, when your natural tendencies cause you to self-sabotage. To flip the script, you have to resolve to change—and believe me, I understand that it's not always easy. But ultimately it can be very rewarding. Now, several years later, I've built my organizations around the concept that good ideas can come from anywhere and that there's great value in collective wisdom—a far cry from where I started, as the above story illustrates. The reason it's so important to focus on being highly attuned to your peers is that it:

1. Shapes your interactions with others
2. Refines your behavior so that your actions support your end goals
3. Creates an awareness of your actions so that you get rid of self-sabotage

You need others' support to build cooperation and teamwork. The ability to foster cooperation and garner others' support requires what some people refer to as *social* or *emotional intelligence*. It requires self-awareness and the ability to be both empathetic and perceptive, and it's a necessary part of gaining the cooperation of others. These characteristics work hand in hand with your hard skills: your intellect, logic, and professional expertise. They help you gain the respect and support of others. Don't underestimate the importance of this kind of intelligence, whether in a personal situation or in the office. Sincere support of your colleagues, friends, and family will serve as a lifeline as you pursue new goals and opportunities. It's a must for flipping the script successfully.

WHY SO EMOTIONAL?

Emotional intelligence (EI) is the ability to perceive, control, and evaluate emotions. It's important because, as Daniel Goleman, who coined the phrase "emotional intelligence" and spent years researching how those skills impact individuals in all settings, will tell you, many companies prize this ability over intellect and technical skill. He found through his research that "For star performance in all jobs, in every field, emotional competence is twice as important as purely cognitive abilities."

In 1999 Cary Cherniss of the Graduate School of Applied and Personal Psychology at Rutgers University set out to prove how emotional intelligence contributes to the bottom line. Here are a few of his findings:

> 1. The US Air Force used the EQ-I [an emotional intelligence test] to select recruiters (the Air Force's front-line HR personnel) and found that the most successful recruiters scored significantly higher in the emotional intelligence competencies of Assertiveness, Empathy, Happiness, and Emotional Self Awareness. The Air Force also found that by using emotional intelligence to select recruiters, they

increased their ability to predict successful recruiters by nearly three-fold. The immediate gain was a saving of $3 million annually. These gains resulted in the Government Accounting Office submitting a report to Congress, which led to a request that the Secretary of Defense order all branches of the armed forces to adopt this procedure in recruitment and selection. (The GAO report is titled "Military Recruiting: The Department of Defense Could Improve Its Recruiter Selection and Incentive Systems," and it was submitted to Congress January 30, 1998. Richard Handley and Reuven Bar-On provided this information.)

2. Experienced partners in a multinational consulting firm were assessed on the EI competencies plus three others. Partners who scored above the median on 9 or more of the 20 competencies delivered $1.2 million more profit from their accounts than did other partners—a 139 percent incremental gain (Boyatzis, 1999).

3. An analysis of more than 300 top-level executives from fifteen global companies showed that six emotional competencies distinguished the brightest stars from just the average. Influence, Team Leadership, Organizational Awareness, Self-confidence, Achievement Drive, and Leadership (Spencer, L. M., Jr., 1997).

4. In jobs of medium complexity (sales clerks, mechanics), top performers in EI are 12 times more productive than those at the bottom and 85 percent more productive than an average performer. In the most complex jobs (insurance salespeople, account managers), a top performer [meaning one who scores high on the EI test] are 127 percent more productive than an average performer (Hunter, Schmidt, & Judiesch, 1990). . . .

5. At L'Oréal, sales agents selected on the basis of certain emotional competencies significantly outsold salespeople selected using the company's old selection procedure. On an annual basis, salespeople selected on the basis of emotional

competence sold $91,370 more than other salespeople did, for a net revenue increase of $2,558,360. Salespeople selected on the basis of emotional competence also had 63% less turnover during the first year than those selected in the typical way (Spencer & Spencer, 1993; Spencer, McClelland, & Kelner, 1997).

So increasing your emotional intelligence is both good for business and a necessary part of flipping the script. To check your EI score, go online; there are many tests available there (they are too long to include in this book). If you are unaware of having a low emotional quotient (EQ), it can really impede your ability to flip. In order to further demonstrate the value of emotional intelligence, let's explore more land mines that people often set for themselves as they endeavor to move ahead in their careers or personal lives. Blaming others, fear of failure, fear of success, making excuses, the desire to win above all else, a lack of self-awareness, and the inability to intuit others' needs and wants are all factors that work against you. To flip the script and reach your goals, you need to abandon these self-defeating behaviors and work some empathy into your repertoire.

I'm not a psychologist, so I can't explain why people do the things they do; what I can do is give you examples of certain practices and open your eyes to their causes and results. I hope to show you exactly what some forms of self-defeating behavior look like and their potential impact, so that you will learn how to put such behavior behind you as you attempt to flip the script.

KNOW-IT-ALL-ISM

As I explained earlier in the story of my embarrassment in Switzerland, as a young salesman I was desperate to prove myself and quickly advance in my first real job. Brash and inexperienced, I suffered from an all too common problem: know-it-all-ism. Know-it-all-ism is an affliction I see in many of the young people I hire each year. Although it's not limited to recent college grads, it is most commonly found among them as a group. Those afflicted with know-it-all-ism believe that although they have very limited experience, they are as smart and knowledgeable as someone who's been doing a similar job for many years. I think this is an issue that many of us have dealt with at one time or another in our careers or our personal lives. In my case, the biggest problem was that I actually knew very little, which is abundantly clear in retrospect. But it wasn't the knowing very little that could have been the potential career killer for me; rather, it was the fact that I'd closed off my mind to learning from my colleagues and especially those senior to me.

My inability to get along with others at work involved quite a few of the land mines I noted above, particularly the overriding desire to win, fear of failure, and an inability to build cooperation. I suppose that many of us feel we are showing weakness if we ask questions or try to be empathetic with our colleagues, but the truth is that when you engage in those behaviors you are building a foundation for future success.

 Flip Tip: The smartest people know what they don't know.

"THE BOSS HATES ME"

One day I got my comeuppance for my know-it-all-ism, and it wasn't pretty. Shortly after I returned from Switzerland, my manager called me into his office. He thoughtfully explained that although he thought I was bright and talented, my insensitivity to others in the office was beginning to cause conflict among my peers. He suggested that I seek some additional interpersonal training and handed me the book *Getting to Yes*. Why would I need to read a book on "getting to yes" when the problem was everyone else's? I thought. They should just do what I told them to do. It was feedback I didn't want to hear.

I was closed to my boss's suggestion and figured this was happening because he hated me. I took one look at the book, rolled my eyes, and promptly threw it into the garbage upon returning to my cubicle.

Many people say that the first reaction to the truth is getting angry. That's exactly what happened. Instead of taking my boss's constructive criticism and thinking about how I could use his advice to improve my interactions with others in the office, I reacted as many of us do: I got angry. It felt better to convince myself that he and everyone else were jealous or that he hated me.

As it happened, I could have learned a very important and useful lesson from that book I foolishly trashed. A big part of "getting to yes" is the idea of *principled* rather than *positional* negotiations. In positional negotiations, you argue your position over someone else's with the goal of coming out on top. That was me. I believed I was right, that my position was the correct one, and that the end goal was for me to win. Principled negotiations require a lot of the emotional intelligence that I didn't possess at the time. That technique takes every party's needs into account. It doesn't mean that you have to compromise on the aspects of a deal that are important to you; it does mean, however, that there is no need to grind the other party into the ground to get your way. That kind of forced win is for the short term, and flipping is about long-term goal achievement. Unfortunately, at the time the short term was all I could see. I didn't have the emotional intelligence to see farther down the road. The fact that in the long term I might need my colleagues, boss, and clients to support me in achieving my goals was lost on me. Understanding and valuing your emotional intelligence can play a pivotal role in the process of flipping your script, primarily because although each flip is an individual process, you have to realize you can't do it alone. You're going to need the help, support, and counsel of others to achieve your flips.

At that time in my career, I did not have vision. I also lacked the much-needed empathy, perceptive ability, and self-knowledge to get along with others as effectively as a good salesman or businessman should. On top of all that, I blamed a lot of people other than myself. I was clueless but not hopeless, and that is an important message for everyone reading this book: you can always turn things around. It was an ideal moment to flip the script, though I didn't realize it at the time.

Rationally, if I'd thought about the situation clearly, my boss didn't hate me. Why would he go through the trouble of sitting me down and giving me the book if he wasn't at some level invested in my becoming a better employee? Clearly, it wasn't his issue; it was mine.

In business, indulging yourself won't get you too far, and I was missing the true picture. Whether my boss liked me or not was actually unimportant. I could stamp my feet all day long, I could indulge myself into believing that the boss and everyone else was against me, but at the end of the day it was up to me to move my career ahead. I had to flip the script and understand that this was just business and not personal. If I wanted to achieve my goals, I needed to take into consideration others' ideas and opinions. I needed their support. I can now see that I was probably making my boss's job more difficult. I had not been respectful or made it clear that there was value for him in helping me achieve my goals.

 Flip Tip: The more you take off your boss's plate, the more valuable you become.

So I shouldn't have been surprised when I called him a month later to get onto his calendar, and his response was "What's your agenda?" My EQ was low, and I had taken every conversation with him as a personal slight rather than a helping hand. Now it was all coming back home. Clearly he saw me as a person will little or no interest in anyone other than myself. That was the beginning of a change. I began to see that you can get only so far if your agenda is always all about you. I was honest and told him that my agenda was that there was a more senior position open at another magazine; it would be a promotion for me, with management responsibility and more money, and I wanted to go for it. I told him I needed his help to allow me to interview for the position. He advised me that he thought I was not ready for a promotion but he would not stand in my way. In retrospect I think he was happy to get rid of me. He was more than fair; though he would not endorse the move, he would not prevent me from trying, which he could have, as company policy dictated that you must have been in your current position for two years or have your manager's approval before moving to a new position.

Though my boss may have viewed me as immature and a lost cause, I wasn't. It's never too late to change for the better. We are all capable of exceeding the expectations of us. That's what this book is about. At that moment I became determined to flip the script. And though I'm sure he didn't realize it—and I didn't act like it at the time—my manager's fairness, professionalism, and emotional intelligence had a tremendous impact on me. He was better to me than I was to him, and it made me want to be better than I was. It was the wake-up call I needed. I went into the interview process for the new job a person in the process of evolving. I was less arrogant and more humble. I was honest about what I didn't know and even went on to talk about some of the lessons I had learned. I began to realize that I could turn myself and my relationships around. I understood for the first time that I didn't need to have all the answers and that I needed others' help and support. I developed greater clarity at work; I began to view things from a more objective business perspective rather than a personal one. Once you separate the personal from business matters, you can control acts of self-sabotage and begin to flip faster.

DON'T TAKE THINGS PERSONALLY

A year later, I found that I would have to put what I had learned into practice during one of the annual reviews in my new position. As it happened, my ex-wife was eight months pregnant with our first child. Over lunch with my manager she and I talked about my career—things I'd been doing well and areas I could improve upon. My review was going well up until the time we started to discuss salary.

I had had a strong year and was outperforming many of my higher-paid colleagues on the sales team. When my manager started to discuss salary increases for the upcoming year, she informed me that I would be getting a 3 percent increase, which was generally on par with most everyone else on the staff. She could probably read the disappointment on my face, because she went on to tell me that she understood it was an important time for me and that as I was expanding my family, money was an important consideration.

That was when I had to think about all that I had learned and separate business from personal. As I saw it, my performance at work had nothing to do with my personal life choices. I was surprised by her comment and diplomatically let her know that though I appreciated her concern for my family, I felt it should not be a factor in my compensation. Whether I had two children or ten was none of the company's concern. I didn't expect my compensation to be tied to my life choices. Did that mean that someone with a large family should get a bigger raise than someone with no children? Or that someone who had a family shouldn't be expected to travel as much as someone who didn't?

Looking back, it was an incredibly valuable lesson. I was able to separate personal from professional. I wanted to be compensated for my performance on the job because I had actually outperformed more senior colleagues that year. My personal choices should not have been factored into the equation or even been a topic of discussion. My manager appreciated what I was saying and, more important, the way I was saying it. I was not criticizing her for her concern and interest; in fact, I let her know that I thought it was nice of her to show an interest in my family. I just needed to move the dialogue back to objective performance and results.

 Flip Tip: When discussing compensation, bring a list of your accomplishments—and always keep the discussion performance-based.

I could see how combining EQ and business acumen could speed my flips. The result was that I received a nice raise, commensurate with my contribution to the company, and I learned a valuable lesson that I have since used when managing people. Separating personal from business matters is the key element in understanding what respect in the office is all about. Respecting others is one thing, but having others respect you can be a completely different story.

The first step in gaining others' respect is realizing how others perceive you.

PERCEPTION IS REALITY

When you are learning to navigate office politics and personalities, one of the most important and first lessons is that perception is reality. When all people know of you is what they see externally, the energy and attitude you give off form a lasting impression. The sad truth is that the axiom "perception is reality" is apt: your behavior determines how other people see you. And how they see you is, in fact, who you are to them in the office environment. Though you need to be true to yourself, you also need to conduct yourself in a manner that supports your stated commitments. How do you want to be perceived? As a professional? Trusted? A consensus builder? Someone with good judgment? Someone who can lead others in the right direction? Employers and coworkers can't see what's inside you; all they can see is what you present to them, and actions always speak louder than words.

HOT TUB?

To illustrate how even the most innocent of actions can be taken the wrong way given the context, I often use the hot-tub analogy. "What is the hot-tub analogy?" you may ask. It's a story that illustrates how in business something can't just *be* right—it has to *look* right and *feel* right to everyone looking on from the outside, as well. What you demonstrate to the outside world becomes reality. And though this case may be extreme, I hope you get the point.

I think that it's commonly understood that one of the most successful ways to build better relationships with your clients is through entertaining them—over dinner, on a golf course, a spa, or in this case, a ski slope. Understanding others' perceptions of you is valuable when conducting yourself in such situations.

In this true story of a close friend of mine who works in the publishing business, a group of coworkers took several clients on a trip to Aspen, Colorado. The advertising directors had spent a long day entertaining the clients on the ski slopes and then took them out for drinks après ski. Finally everyone headed back to the large house that they were sharing. All the hotels were booked, and renting a house had seemed like a good idea at the time. It had been a fun and productive business day. Relationships with the clients had been formed or strengthened, the sales team had bonded, and the group was having a good time. That evening, after a long and exhausting day on the slopes, bones and muscles tired, everyone, including two managers, one sales executive, and one client decided to jump into the hot tub. Everyone in the group went back to his or her respective room, put on a swimsuit, and headed out to the hot tub.

Several weeks later, one of the employees who had attended the trip and participated in the hot-tub session was dismissed for padding his expenses; it was considered being fired "for cause," and as a result he was given no severance. Through his lawyer, he countercharged that he had felt uncomfortable two weeks earlier, when he had felt pressured to take off his shirt and get into the hot tub with his boss. He wanted compensation, or he would sue the company.

As the company lawyers explained to my friend, the company wanted to settle the claim and avoid litigation. Even though it knew, based on witnesses' statements, that his claim was erroneous, unfortunately the situation still didn't look right. The lawyer went on to explain: Imagine that you are in a court of law and that one employee whom you loved and had at one time thought was a great employee was now on the stand. He is now a problem—for you particularly. He has brought a lawsuit against you claiming sexual harassment. As you sit in front of the court and respond to the prosecutors, the dialogue could sound something like this:

"So, Mr. X, you were out with Mr. Y and Mr. Z, who reported to you, correct?"

"Yes," you answer.

"And you had been drinking?"

"Yes."

"And what were you wearing?"

"A swimsuit."

The prosecutor continues, "Let me get this straight. You were with an employee of the firm who reports to you, and you'd been drinking. Then you're in the hot tub with that employee with barely any clothes on?" "Correct," you respond. You would be considered guilty regardless of what had actually happened in the hot tub. In the end the company, which the complainant's lawyers saw as having "deep pockets," settled with the ex-employee to avoid a protracted legal battle. It seems unfair, right? But it demonstrates that you can't control what others are going to do, but you can control the situations you put yourself into. Had the managers decided not to go into the hot tub, the man would have had no case. That's the unfortunate thing: your actions can't just *be* right, they have to *look* right to the outside world.

Flipping means managing all aspects of a situation, including the internal and external. I think the above example illustrates why it's often hard for us to face that reality and why we often make excuses. The managers felt they hadn't done anything wrong, and they certainly had not harassed the employee, but a successful flip requires that we not confuse our motives with what the world sees. To move our goals forward, we have to be mature enough to recognize that perception, unfortunately, is reality. That is business, and our actions and behavior shape how others see us and see our potential for growth. The good news is that we can control in ways both big and small how the world sees us. For example, every month when I meet with our top executives I plan in advance and always wear my best suit, make sure my shoes are polished, and wear a new tie. I know my exposure to them is limited, so I want to present the best image of me. But no matter how many times I use the example of the hot-tub story, inevitably there are people who just don't get it. They see the world as unjust and continue to make excuses. They can't see that it's their excuses that are holding them back and preventing them from flipping their scripts.

EXCUSE ME

One of the worst ways you can sabotage yourself is to be defensive and make excuses for your behavior. Making excuses seems to have risen to the level of an art form. But making excuses for yourself to your manager, team, family, and friends doesn't help them understand or forgive what it was you did or didn't do; it just underscores your failing.

The need to make excuses has been attributed to everything from our DNA (I have my father's temperament) to our upbringing and education (that's what the nuns taught me) to our influences (that's what we did in my first job). People cling to those origins as though they are defenseless against the urge to justify their actions—no matter the circumstance or the ridiculousness of the excuse itself. The truth is that although perhaps you have been influenced by past experiences and your natural reaction is to make up some kind of explanation, you can choose to do otherwise. Dr. Wayne Dyer has written many books on the topic of motivation, including *Excuses Begone!: How to Change Lifelong, Self-Defeating Thinking Habits,* each of which has been turned into a special on National Public Television. Dyer has spent decades examining the aspects of ourselves that keep us from achieving fulfillment. One of the root causes is the need to make excuses. That act may absolve you of a wrongdoing or failure in your own mind, but in fact what you are doing is rejecting any type of accountability, and, going back to the notion of perception being reality, it makes you look bad in both personal and professional settings.

Let's examine this practice a little more deeply. What happens if you're never accountable? You can never learn from your mistakes. You can never grow in experience and understanding. You remain stuck in a relationship that has lost its luster, a job that has turned into a dead end, or a state of desperation where you can't see the opportunities that are passing you by. You have eliminated—or at least greatly jeopardized—your ability to flip the script.

In his book, Dr. Dyer acknowledges that although you may be influenced by your experiences and by those around you, you have the ability to reject the desire to make excuses. Dyer emphasizes that "the one and only place that your excuses originated was in you." He advises, "to live a totally excuse-free life, you must be willing to state: 'I adopted these behaviors—I chose all of it and I take full responsibility for any and all excuses that I've engaged in.'"

Once you perform this act of contrition, you are ready to deal with the really hard question: Why all the excuses to begin with? What motivates you to attempt explaining and overexplaining your actions, feelings, and words?

Has a friend, your sister, or an employee ever offered a truly inane excuse for why he or she failed to show up at a restaurant or meeting on time? How about why he or she needed to leave work early? Why a project didn't get finished on time? And, of course, probably the most-used excuse of all: why they won't be coming into work that day? I actually prefer someone to simply say, "You know, I'm really exhausted" or "I didn't get any sleep last night, I'll make it up this weekend by coming in and still keep our deadlines." As a manager, I would be satisfied with that response because what the person is doing is being honest and taking accountability for the work that needs to be done. But devising some excuse that will fool someone else is disrespectful to both yourself and the person you are trying to mislead. And as discussed previously, you can't flip your script if you don't have respect for yourself and others. Over the years I've heard so many excuses, too many to count—many of them from bright and talented individuals who don't see how making excuses is holding them back. Two stories in particular come to mind. The first is about a woman named Lisa, who was extremely ambitious. She could turn on the charm and was always trying to convince her manager that she was ready to be promoted. She always said the right things, so finally the manager decided to put her in charge of a project. The project consisted of managing a small sales and marketing team and had to be completed in two weeks. Now that she was in charge of managing a team, it quickly became apparent that her words did not align with her actions. Regardless of where the team was in completing the assignments, she left work every day at 4 P.M. As the day progressed, invariably the group she was managing needed answers to questions. The problem was that if it was after 4 p.m., she was nowhere to be found. She didn't tell anyone she was leaving. She never told her manager that she had some personal conflict that would explain her actions. As the deadline approached, the team was dreadfully behind schedule. Lisa's manager confronted her; she told her that the team needed her and she was letting herself and the team down. She questioned her, asking if she had not wanted this opportunity. But rather than owning up and taking responsibility for the mismanagement of the project—seeing this moment as a growth opportunity—or admitting that the project was perhaps more work than she had expected and a promotion was not what she truly wanted, Lisa made lame excuses. The excuse she came up with when confronted was that she lived on the Upper West Side of Manhattan and took a spin class at six o'clock. She went on to explain, "This is the only time I do something for me, and if I don't leave by four p.m., it becomes really hard to catch a cab uptown once rush-hour traffic starts." When the manager heard that, she wasn't sure if Lisa was making it up or, worse, if it was the truth and she actually believed that it was a justifiable reason. Either way, her inability to take responsibility and stop making excuses had stopped her flip—a new opportunity—dead in its tracks.

The other story involves an employee, Sheila, whom I hired when I was the publisher of *Details* magazine. She was a temp, and her job was to answer the phones in the marketing department. It became obvious early on that she was not serious about her career prospects at *Details*. She hardly ever picked up the phone line she was assigned to answer, and the calls would bounce to other assistants' desks. As I walked the floors daily, I almost never saw her at her desk. She would be busy talking with the male editors or standing gossiping by the other assistants' desks. And though I have to take responsibility for not dealing with the situation immediately, it seemed easier to try to "manage her to success" than to make an immediate change in personnel. I called her in and told her she needed to be more proactive and take her job seriously. She said that the phone system was complicated but assured me that she would step up her game.

The next week I saw her sitting at her desk, the phone in one ear, talking. I was proud of myself, thinking "She just needed a bit of direction." That feeling lasted only about two days, when the head of the marketing department came in to advise me that we needed to move Sheila out; the marketing team had realized that it was not getting any calls. "How can that be?" I inquired. Apparently, Sheila was speaking into the phone and doing what looked like taking messages, but when people's spouses or friends tried calling the number, they would get a dead line. The manager questioned Sheila, who made the excuse that she was afraid of the phone system and it was just too complicated. So rather than ask for help, she had decided to just unplug the phone. For several days she had just sat there and pretended to take messages. I couldn't make this up if I tried.

Why do we do such things? Why do we engage in a frustrating, annoying, and ineffective way of dealing with our own shortcomings and interacting with others? Earlier in this chapter, I stressed the importance of respect. Such behavior is thoroughly the opposite. You are not showing your spouse, boss, or mother respect by covering your behavior with an excuse, however clever it may be. Think tanks and institutions have conducted studies that address this very behavior and found that the motivations for excuse making vary wildly. Some people say they fear success; others fear failure; some want to impress another person; others want to lower others' expectations.

We may think that making excuses will somehow excuse us from our responsibilities at work and in our personal lives, but it never does. It may for the moment, but, like a bad cavity, responsibility doesn't go away, and the longer you avoid dealing with the truth and your responsibilities, the more painful the end result may be. At work, when you make excuses, you jeopardize your credibility, the chance for honest communication, and your ability to flip the script.

 Flip Tip: Don't do anything you'll have to find an excuse for.

Changing such behavior isn't easy, but it can be done. *The New York Times* published an incredibly interesting piece on just this topic called "Some Protect the Ego by Working on Their Excuses Early." In it the journalist described legions of people from all walks of life—students and professionals—who practice this form of self-sabotage:

> . . . genuine excuse artisans—and there are millions of them—don't wait until after choking to practice their craft. They hobble themselves, in earnest, before pursuing a goal or delivering a performance. Their excuses come preattached: I never went to class. I was hung over at the interview. I had no idea what the college application required.

The researchers cited in the article all agreed that this type of "handicapping" behavior should be avoided altogether. But like anything else, the more the excuser gets away with justifying his shortcomings, the more common the behavior becomes. It becomes a vicious cycle. And although people may think they are getting away with such behavior, like that bad cavity, I wonder, will it eventually start to hurt them?

Are you a habitual excuse maker? Are you fearful of overpromising and underdelivering? Do your actions fall short of the goals you've stated to your boss or wife? Is this because you lack the drive to follow through? If you recognize any of these tendencies in yourself, Dr. Dyer has practical advice for ridding yourself of this destructive behavior. He recommends asking yourself a few probing questions. The four cited below will get you on your way to eliminating this self-sabotaging behavior:

1. **Are my worst fears true? Or am I seeing the situation clearly?**
    Does my boss really hate me? In the example I gave earlier in this chapter, we established that this wasn't the case.
2. **Where are the excuses coming from?**
    In my case, excuses were a reaction to being confronted with criticism—the fact that I still had room to improve

my performance and develop further. The need to make an excuse arose from anger from a bruised ego.

3. **What's the payoff?**
   Maybe making an excuse fed my ego and shielded me from the knowledge that I did not, in fact, know everything. But what did I lose? What do you gain or lose by making excuses?

4. **What would my life be like if I couldn't use these excuses?**
   What would life look like if I were honest and self-reflective?

Stopping the excuses and accepting the knowledge and experience of my peers and managers forced me to take some responsibility for my actions, and as a result I began to grow in emotional intelligence—one thing built on the other, and soon the process of flipping became easier and quicker. Making excuses is one way to sabotage your career, but it's not the only way. Over the years I've witnessed countless other acts of self-sabotage. Let's take a look at some of the more common examples and some easy ways to manage them on your way to flipping.

AVOIDING SELF-SABOTAGE AT WORK

Though it's important to foster good relationships and camaraderie in the office, sometimes this is easier said than done. Though you may be evolving in your style and behavior to grow and flip, that doesn't mean that everyone else is on the same path. Working closely with colleagues is like learning to live in your dorm freshman year all over again. Personalities, close quarters, and different backgrounds and values are all fertile ground for the many types of problematic relationships that can arise between colleagues. I'd like to offer some guidance based on my experience navigating some of those relationships. Here are just a few of the ways I've seen people derail their flips over the years and some simple ways to help deal with common office issues.

"Oh, No, You Didn't"

Do you have a colleague who says "no" to every idea you have? There are many ways to deal with office naysayers, but I have found two that work particularly well. First, if you don't have to work directly with a person, be smart; don't preview your ideas to him or her—take them to your boss or to collaborators who will give you constructive criticism or good advice. If you do have to work alongside naysayers, you should: (1) Face them head-on. Sit down together and hear them out. Just because they are naysayers doesn't mean that all of their ideas are bad ones; they may have valid and helpful opinions. Once you've heard them out, you can say, "We have a difference of opinion on this matter, but I've decided that what's best for the organization is _____. What I really need to know now is that you're on board with me." Then solicit their acceptance by asking, "Are you?" (2) Enlist their help; I recently encountered a great example of how this can work effectively. A friend of mine, Lynn, owns a small chain of hair and beauty salons in northern New Jersey. As her business grew, she wanted to create a more unified corporate culture among the salons, so she decided to create a dress code for the stylists and employees: black clothes only. It was met with great resistance by many of the stylists—and because hair salons live and die by their stylists' clients, Lynn felt she was in a tough spot. She wanted to counteract the building mutiny and avoid the loss of her top stylists. So she called me for advice.

I advised her to find the one or two most vocal stylists, the chief naysayers at each salon, and schedule a lunch with them all together. I suggested that she praise them for their leadership skills and tell them what her business objectives were; she needed to explain *why* she wanted to change the dress code. I then told her to enlist their help and ask them what they would do to address and overcome the challenge. She did as we discussed and was surprised to find that good ideas began to circulate at the luncheon. Suggestions included: the company could give a small stipend to help offset the cost of new clothes for the first three months, deducting the loan as a percentage of their sales, or it could provide well-made black T-shirts for the employees to wear. By the end of the lunch the group had come up with a plan. Lynn had enlisted the largest voices in the group and made her issue their issue, and they had found a way to work through the problem. Now you can walk into any of her salons and see a smiling staff all dressed in black.

 Flip Tip: When dealing with "Dr. No"s, hear them out and enlist their help.

That's Company Property

From email to social networking sites, you need to keep your private and public worlds separate, and, more important, you need to know what belongs to you and what belongs to the company. Blurring those worlds is the kind of mistake that far too many businesspeople make, and it's an easy way to sabotage your career.

Any printed material or online communication that is produced as a function of your job is the property of the company. Though this is common sense, today many of us use the company phone as a personal number or the company email account to send personal email. The line between what's the company's and what's yours has become increasingly blurred, and for some this confusion can come at a great cost. A shocking example of this happened recently at a friend's accounting firm. My friend Eric is a general manager at one of the big multinational accounting firms. One day he was called in to the human resources office. It appeared that the husband of one of his employees had visited HR. The man had made the claim that his wife was possibly being sexually harassed by her boss. This was an unusual claim to be made by a spouse rather than the employee. Regardless of who made the claim, it needed to be taken very seriously. In the company's opinion, her boss was a solid performer and rising star. He reported directly to Eric. When Eric heard the news, he was shocked. He had never seen any discriminatory behavior by the manager, with whom he had worked for years. It seemed so out of character. In fact, he would have guessed that the manager and the employee had a positive, friendly working relationship. Indeed they did; it was too friendly. In the course of responding to the claim, Human Resources secretly went through all the manager's emails and text messages without his knowledge, which it had the right to do since the messages had been sent using company equipment, and found that the manager and the employee were having a consensual sexual relationship. Some of the emails were quite explicit. Human Resources told the husband that it did not appear that the relationship was one of a discriminatory nature. Both the manager and the employee were called in and asked directly about the situation. Unfortunately, both denied the existence of any relationship, not knowing that the company had proof. In the end, the company was forced to terminate both employees.

 Flip Tip: If you didn't pay for it, it ain't yours. Keep work devices strictly business.

When Facebook Isn't Your Friend

This brings me to a topic that all of us need to pay close attention to: exposing your thoughts and deeds on the Internet via social networking sites. I know that you can't always control all of the information that exists about you online, but you can make a conscious choice about what you post and who sees it. This is particularly relevant in the case of Facebook. In doing some research, I was disturbed to find how many stories there were about people who had lost their jobs because of using Facebook. It seems that the Internet is filled with countless people who post negative things about their boss or workplace, even when their boss is their Facebook friend. I'm dumbfounded by this type of behavior, and I just can't understand how it happens, but it does happen over and over again. In fact, there's even a Facebook page dedicated to people who lost their jobs because of Facebook!

I recently heard a disturbing story about an employee who had called in sick and who felt the repercussions of what she posted on her Facebook wall. The employee called her manager on a Monday morning, complaining of the stomach flu, raspy voice and all. She said she would not be able to come in and that she knew the proposal for her tech account was due but asked if her manager or someone else in the department could complete it. Remember what we talked about earlier, about how excuses can derail your flips? Well, that's what happened in this case because this employee was "friends" with many of the other women in the department and one of them decided to show the manager the posts on the employee's Facebook page, which included NO WORK TODAY. I NEED MORE BEACH and LESS BULLSHIT. SEE YOU IN THE SUN. And that's exactly what she got—more time in the sun, because that was her last day of work at the company.

 Flip Tip: Not everyone who can see your postings is a "friend"; edit accordingly.

THE PARENT TRAP

You may have heard of the "parent trap," but the parent trap I'm referring to isn't the lighthearted Disney movie of the same name; it is set when we blame our failures, shortcomings, or lack of follow-through on our families or upbringing. To flip, we need to beat the parent trap and not let our upbringing and things that happened in the past brand us for today and the future. Before we consider ways to eradicate this behavior, let's consider why many of us tend to blame so much on our childhoods.

The psychologist Dr. Raymond Havlicek, who specializes in parenting and family psychology, explains it this way: "This focus on psychosocial predestination has caused many to lose sight of their own potential to reshape their lives. Understanding the possibility for personal redirection and growth is most important because many have discovered that the source of their adult adjustment problems and/or distress is a painful childhood, without knowing that anything can be done to change; the dye [*sic*] has been cast, so to speak. This painful self-realization has caused some to believe that a new and better life is not possible." That is why you have to learn to flip the script, because a new life *is* possible. One of the ways of explaining our tendency to fixate on past experiences is something called memetics.

The field of memetics is like genetics in that "memes are the basic building blocks of our minds and culture, in the same way that genes are the basic building blocks of biological life." Richard Brodie, who is a pioneer in this field, refers to memes as the "virus of the mind," because memes, or memories, carry around the baggage of our past experiences, including our upbringing. A meme has no physical presence as a gene or DNA does, but Brodie describes it as "a thought, belief, or attitude in your mind that can be spread to and from other people's minds." They are the stories and realities we create in our minds around our memories. In his book *Excuses Begone!*, which I mentioned earlier, Dr. Wayne Dyer pointed out that memes are dangerous because once they are in your mind they can affect your behavior consciously or unconsciously, spreading like a virus and making escaping the parent trap that much more difficult. Earlier, I talked about people making excuses related to their childhood as being a big part of their inability to flip the script. This is a problem that many of us face in business. It's almost as though we're hardwired to blame our failings, lack of attention, or follow-through on our families and upbringing. Of course, there are positive memes—good habits or lessons we've learned from our past—but they don't hold us back. We need to get rid of all toxic influences that cause problems. Too often we use memes as another way to make excuses for ourselves, rather than change our behavior.

How does laying blame on our parents or families have a direct effect on our personal and professional lives, and why can it be so dangerous? Over the years I have worked with people who have blamed their parents for everything from their poor communication skills, dysfunctional relationships, destructive habits, and irrational behaviors to their fat body and poor eating habits. Recently, a friend at work was complaining to me about some of her dad's questionable behavior. The exact details aren't important except to say that she ended her tirade with a line I've heard a million times, from people both inside and outside work: "He should have known better. He's the parent, for God's sake!" Although this seemed to make sense, the person I was talking to was a midlevel manager in the company—and was thirty-two years old. She was old enough to be a parent herself. Did she think that when you have kids or reach a certain age, a magic "perfection" powder falls on you? An even bigger issue was that she began to apply the logic to her attitude toward her boss, the new authority figure in her life.

You would think that all of us should be able to rise above the impact that our upbringing has on us, but it is harder than it appears. But as I've mentioned throughout the book, it's essential that we learn to separate our business and personal lives. Although we need to recognize that how we were raised has and will have a direct effect on our values and interactions at work, to flip the script we have to be able to separate negative fallout from our childhood from our current work and personal life. It gets in the way, and in my friend's case her feelings about her father's parenting were coloring her work situation. She transferred the notion that parents are all-knowing to her boss. She expected her boss to be equally infallible, which caused issues at work, because when the boss could not read her moods or know what she was thinking, she was easily frustrated. The problem is that my colleague wasn't a thirteen-year-old kid who can afford to expect her parents or any authority figure to be able to rise above human frailties and pettiness. She was an adult, and although her logic—that her father or the boss should always take the higher road—might have carried a tremendous amount of weight when she was a teen, it had lost a lot of its potency now that she was in her thirties. She was the one who needed to grow up.

Sure, we would all like our parents or coworkers to be faultless creatures worthy of our highest admiration. Who wouldn't want them to always act in our best interest, to have no agendas, and to be shining examples of maturity, morality, love, support, and reason? We all know, however, that this is rarely the way the parent/child dynamic plays out. At some point, we must move on and stop blaming our parents for life's failures and frustrations.

Understanding that there is a parent trap and learning to break the cycle is an important step in understanding what holds us back—what keeps us from flipping the script and seeing new opportunities. An unresolved parent trap can be an endless cycle. Always hungry, it can provide a never-ending supply of excuses and blame as to why you are not living up to or achieving your personal best. Just like the act of "blamestorming" in the office, which I mentioned earlier in the book, many people shift blame to their families to avoid personal accountability. But that is a dangerous, self-sabotaging behavior.

BLAME IS LIKE CANDY

Candy may taste good going down, but too much of it winds up making you feel sick to your stomach. Similarly, though it may offer some comfort in the short term, it's pointless to blame your current bad behavior or lack of success on your parents—or anyone else, for that matter. What's standing between you and success right now is *you*. Not your folks, not your history, just you. I'm not suggesting that you deny your past, but I am advising that you refuse to live there because it just might kill your future. Ask yourself what patterns of behavior, what trust issues, what authority issues you are bringing to work with you every day. How might they be keeping you from moving forward? They might be more insidious than you think.

You are responsible for both your current reality and your future. To be able to flip the script, you need to be able to move on—to turn the page. It's not about what others do or don't deserve; it's about what *you* deserve. Here is an example of how dealing with your role in the parent trap can play out at work. Last year I was sitting down with two top managers at one of the magazines I managed who were in similar-level positions. They were both talented and hardworking, but they needed to develop their initiative and grow in their abilities to problem solve and think critically. If they were given a specific task, they could complete it effectively, but if they needed to initiate the creative process, they froze. That was clearly holding them back. Without improvement they could not move to the next level.

I decided to have conversations with them individually and lay out where I thought they needed to concentrate their efforts. Their responses were telling and underscored my point that even highly effective individuals can be hamstrung by their pasts.

It was a fascinating case study because I sat each one down individually, giving them similar talks and advice. What's interesting is that each had totally different responses to my well-intentioned advice. One took immediate responsibility when I asked, "Why do you think you are not problem solving on your own?" His response was "It makes no difference what I think, what matters is that you are my boss, and if you don't think I am, then I need to change it. What do you suggest I do?"

Compare that to the second manager, who, when I asked the same question, "Why do you think you are not problem solving more on your own?" essentially blamed me, stating "You never gave me the chance. People don't come to me because they go to you, and if I were in charge and promoted, I would be problem solving more." Wrong answer.

It was as if she believed that you're a leader when someone puts you at the front of the line as opposed to actually leading, which in fact is the thing that puts you at the front of the line. In this situation she was the child and I was the parent. It was my fault. She just as easily could have been saying "You didn't make me do my homework. That's why I failed." The influence of the parent trap can be subtle or direct, but it affects our interactions at work and in our lives daily—if you let it. To deal with it, you first have to realize it's there and then think about how to make lemonade out of lemons. What I mean is that beating the parent trap may be as easy as changing perspective.

SUCCESS IS PERSPECTIVE: DON'T DISS DYSFUNCTION

Each of us has our own unique perspective, or "take," on any given situation. I'm sure you've had the experience of sitting in a room with another person and thinking you are both having the same conversation, but in truth the only thing you agree on later is that you were both physically in the same room at the same time. In fact, each of you took away a completely different meaning from the conversation. When illustrating this point, I tell people that a physical manifestation may help get your hands around the concept. Try this: imagine that you and I are sitting in a room in two chairs facing each other, having a conversation. Behind me is a picture, and behind you is a window. Though we both agree that we were in that specific room at that specific time, our perspectives and what we can see are totally different. You can see whatever the picture is, and I can see whatever is happening outside the window. We are both correct. This is true internally as well, as each one of us brings our past perspectives with us.

What happens if the perspective you bring is negative and shapes what you see? What if we decided to change our perspective and, rather than concentrating on all the things we weren't given or the chances we didn't have, instead saw them as positives? What if we took our dysfunctional growing up and, rather than trying to escape it, embraced it? We would begin to perceive the gaps in our childhood or lack of attention from our parents as something that could propel us forward rather than hold us back. There are many individuals who have done just that, successful people who have taken challenges from their past and, rather than lamenting, have used them as a source of energy and drive. If you're looking for inspiration, read on.

The following two stories illustrate how two current top CEOs flipped their scripts. Their stories are extreme and prove to us all that no matter who you are or where you come from, you have the ability to create success.

Ursula M. Burns, CEO, Xerox

Xerox's new CEO, Ursula Burns, graduated from some of New York's most prestigious schools, including Columbia University, where she received a master of science in mechanical engineering. Based on the incredible success she's achieved, you would never know that early in life, she endured a difficult childhood in the projects of New York City.

As a child, Burns lived in the Baruch Houses, low-income housing where "the common denominator and great equalizer was poverty." Because of the rough surroundings, Burns's mother sent all three of her children to Catholic school so that they would get "a good education and be safe." Her mother, Olga, cared for Burns and her two siblings on her own. To keep the family afloat, Olga took in ironing and ran a day care center from their apartment.

Burns gives her mother, Olga, a great deal of credit for her own success. To her, Olga was a shining example of grit and determination. In 2010, at a YWCA Women Empowering Women event, Burns shared that she had learned much from her mother, the most important lesson being not to let your environment brand you. About her mother Burns said, "She gave us courage. She gave us will and love. I can still hear her telling me that where you are is not who you are. If you're in a bad place, it's only temporary and shouldn't change the core value of what you can bring to the world."

Burns is a living example of her mother's words that "where you are is not *who* you are." She didn't let the difficulties of her early years diminish her determination and in fact found courage in her mother's example. Burns is far from the impoverished neighborhood she grew up in on Delancey Street in New York City and is the first African-American woman to head a Fortune 500 company.

Even today Burns remains humble concerning her success and sees that there is much more she needs to do to advance her career and promote growth at Xerox. At the company's annual meeting, she told her audience that within days of being appointed CEO she was also named to a number of prestigious lists, but she shrugged off these honors, saying "It's all about growth. It's all about getting bigger." That seems to be a quintessential reaction from Burns, who takes a humble yet no-nonsense approach to her achievements.

Li Ka-shing, CEO, Hutchison Whampoa Limited (Hong Kong)

Can you imagine what you would need to do to earn the nickname "Superman"? Well, that's how Li Ka-shing is referred to in his adopted homeland, Hong Kong, where he is widely known for his business acumen and deal-making ability. The chairman of Hutchison Whampoa Limited and Cheung Kong (Holdings) Limited, Li is the richest man of East Asian descent and one of the wealthiest men in the world, with a net worth of $26 billion.

But Li did not start out on top. He was born in a relatively poor village in China in 1928; his father was a teacher who instilled in Li the importance of education. In 1940, when Li was twelve, the Japanese began bombing his village as World War II got under way, and the family moved to Hong Kong. For a while they lived with Li's wealthy uncle, but for the most part the family struggled. Shortly after they arrived in Hong Kong, Li's father died of tuberculosis, and Li was forced to drop out of high school at fifteen to support the family. After his father's death, Li began selling plastic watchbands and belts and then moved on to plastic flowers. After a few years, through hard work and a strict discipline of saving, Li was able to run the factory that made plastic flowers and later bought it in 1950. That was the start of many investments and business deals that would take Li into a variety of businesses in Asia and around the world. His early experiences also instilled in him a deep desire to give back. He founded his own philanthropic organization and has contributed $10 billion of his own money to its initiatives.

In a *Wall Street Journal* article, Li was asked about his philanthropic endeavors, because China is widely known to prohibit such activities. Li has had great courage in creating his foundation and visibly supporting education efforts in China. When asked if his child-hood had any influence on his philanthropic work, Li responded:

> When I was a young boy, before I turned 10, I had already seen the war in my hometown. The air force bombed the city. Many people were poor.
>
> After we moved to Hong Kong in 1940, many people from the mainland were in Hong Kong. It was very difficult to get an education. My father wasn't earning enough money to support me to go to school. I tried to find time to study by myself, but I went to full-time work when I was 12 years old.
>
> Later on, my father got tuberculosis. I realized that when you are less fortunate how much support you need. So when I started my own business in 1950, I tried to spend money to help the poor.

Li is a terrific example of someone who flipped the script. He didn't let a lack of formal education or even his incredibly tragic circumstances deter him. He didn't spend time blaming others or sit-ting at his desk waiting for change. He made success happen. And so can you.

LEMONADE, ANYONE?

Realizing that our childhood may not have been perfect, the question is, how can we get past it? To move beyond the parent trap and stop blaming others, I've created a quick four-step method to help change perspective, to begin to see others as profoundly human, and to make peace with their and our limitations:

Step 1: Empathize.

If you are challenged by behavior that took place in the past, you don't need to make excuses or turn a blind eye when one or both of your parents, family, or friends behaves reprehensibly, but you do need to understand—on a deep, profound level—that your parents, family, and friends are human beings and not superheroes. You must take the best from your parents, family, and friends and improve on it to make yourself better. Think of it this way: you can borrow the best of what you like in others rather than fixating on their worst traits. So write down ten things you like and value about those who are closest to you. When issues pop up that get under your skin, refer to that list and remember the good as well as the bad. Flip the negatives into positives; you will see when you flip them that you will begin to create empathy for others as well as to increase the empathy of others toward you.

Step 2: Recognize.

In step 2, you must recognize that your childhood or past experiences do not represent your current life and move on. Whatever situation or hurts you may have experienced are in the past. The past, like the future, does not exist; it is not real. It is only in your mind. You can't touch it. It's only a memory. And we have the power to control whether we choose to dwell on that memory or not. Recognize that the only thing that is real is the present. And that today, in the present, you—not anyone else—are in control of yourself. Knowing that, what are you going to do with that power?

Step 3: Make peace.

In step 3, to move forward, you must make peace. Blaming your parents or others for your station in life is futile. Make a vow to become a better person and/or parent than your parents were. This can be a very powerful motivating tool that can spur you on to bigger and better things. By acknowledging the faults and failings of your upbringing, not only can you make a promise to yourself to succeed in spite of your upbringing, but you can vow to be a better person because of it!

Step 4: Move on.

Move on. I bet you would be hard pressed to find anyone who had a perfect, drama-free childhood or upbringing. Almost everybody has had crosses to bear. Granted, some crosses are much heavier than others, but the point is that everyone knows what it's like to deal with pain and sorrow. Some of the most successful, vibrant people have started out life in dire straits. Many famous, productive, and ultra-happy people are those who learned to channel their hurt and rage early in life and used it to transform themselves. Know that it's never too late, regardless of the issue or the problem. What are the good traits you've developed as a result of early hardships? Are you su-perorganized because your house was a mess while you were growing up? Are you resourceful because you had to be at too young an age? How can you find the good in difficult circumstances? Constantly ask yourself these kinds of questions, and you will be pushing yourself to achieve new goals.

LOVING YOUR FRECKLES

Once you start to work through those steps, loving your freckles—that is, accepting the imperfections—becomes much easier. We'll discuss how learning to be your biggest advocate and not your harshest critic can have a dramatic effect on your ability to flip your script. Whatever your past, you can't let your upbringing brand you. A posi-tive and necessary step in our evolution is the need to accept who we are. This is sometimes easier said than done. Many books have been written about the importance of self-acceptance, but how you actu-ally achieve this is an open question. I think that at some point, we all come to terms with life's tribulations, but in the meantime what do you do to manage the hand you're dealt and make certain it's not stopping you from flipping?

One of the easiest things organizational psychologists recom-mend doing is to simply remove negative thoughts from your think-ing. In his book *Hard Optimism,* Price Pritchett points out that although many studies show the advantages of positive thinking, few people consider the fact that "nonnegative thinking has far greater benefits." So maybe, though we can't fool ourselves that our past was great, we can choose not to dwell on how bad it was. We've all probably had the experience of trying to force ourselves to be optimistic—and it never works, does it? The more you force it, the worse you feel. Instead, you should try to eliminate negative thoughts by using what I call purposeful distraction. Purposeful distraction is when you consciously try to distract yourself. I think we've all had the experience at a cocktail party when you start talking to someone and the conversation is going nowhere. You excuse yourself and move on, right? Purposeful distraction is learning to do that with yourself. For example, if you feel yourself going to dark and negative places, excuse yourself and change your thought patterns; think about something else. Rather than dwelling on them and letting negative emotions build, tell yourself you can think about them later. Distract your mind momentarily; force yourself to think about something else that is happening in the meeting. As a result, you will notice that your negative emotions and feelings decline. By the time you revisit the issue later, the intensity of what you felt will have diminished, allowing you to view it more objectively.

 Flip Tip: When you feel you are going to a negative place, practice purposeful distraction.

TRY VISUALIZATION

If distraction doesn't work, try visualization. Sports psychologists encourage athletes to run their "best-plays reel" through their heads whenever faced with a challenge. That way, a pitcher, for example, can visualize moments when he was successful and gain confidence from those memories. This technique also helps reduce panic and stops negative feelings from setting in. Recently business professionals have been seeking the help of sports psychologists for this kind of problem. In an October 13, 2010, *Wall Street Journal* article, "Slumping at Work," the relationship between sports and business slumps was examined. The article listed equally applicable reasons for why athletes and executives can sometimes lose sight of positive self-acceptance and focus on negatives—which can lead to professional slumps both on and off the field.

The article listed several ways in which a critical attitude and lack of self-acceptance can cause poor performance, including:

- Fear of repeating past failures
- Dwelling on past mistakes
- Loss of confidence
- Overthinking the next move or play and choking or freezing
- Overtraining in sports, burning out on the job
- Forgetting your original purpose or attraction to your sport or job
- Resurfacing of past fears arising from psychological trauma or injury

Recently I've witnessed firsthand how lack of self-acceptance can derail one from the process of flipping. A colleague of mine was promoted to associate publisher of a large women's magazine. This internal promotion made him second in command at the magazine. It was a big job. Though relatively young, in his early thirties, Ed is a smart, ambitious, dedicated, and resourceful executive. Considering all this, I was surprised when I ran into him in the waiting room of an advertising agency. He looked drawn and tired, and the light that had been ever present in his eyes was missing.

"How are you doing?" I asked.

"Drowning," he replied with a shrug.

"Okay. Want to talk about it?" I inquired.

"Not here, but yeah, can we grab lunch sometime?"

When we met for lunch, it was like talking to a different Ed. The last time we had run into each other, he had been energetic and pushing for the promotion. He knew the magazine and had worked there for several years in a lower-level management position with success. I asked if what was bothering him was just the immediate pressure from the transition to the larger responsibility. We can all feel this at times, and we adjust; such feelings are often temporary, and things get better with time. But I could see by Ed's responses that what was going on was more than just temporary. He told me that he was so worn out that at the end of the day he just climbed into bed and crashed, rarely meeting friends for dinner or drinks. He said he was having a hard time getting out of bed in the morning and felt constantly exhausted. This was a far cry from the energetic, funny, stay-till-the-last-drink Ed that I knew.

As we started to dive deeper into the issues plaguing him, I asked when he had started to feel like this. He said that initially he had been excited about the promotion, the new title, and the increased income. But he felt he had made some missteps early on; a few bad calls had led to the magazine losing some smaller accounts. It was nothing catastrophic, but the internal pressure of his new position combined with those small failures had caused him to start to question his abilities and opened a box of self-doubt.

It appeared that the box was growing larger as the pressure and weight of driving the magazine's sales and revenue process were now resting squarely on his shoulders. It also didn't help his self-confidence that the magazine's publisher had pushed him to be more organized and had made him defend a few of his decisions in public meetings. Ed said that when he went home he just thought over and over about all the mistakes he had made. He was frustrated because now, with some separation and reflection, he could easily see better decisions he might have made, but it was too late to go back and change anything. He lay awake at night, wondering if his boss was regretting his decision to promote him. All those factors had him clearly focused on negative thinking, and that was putting him into a slump. He told me, "I just don't think I can do this job." He was close to giving in to self-doubt. He needed to be snapped out of his negative downward spiral.

I listened, and when he was finished I asked him a question: "Have you done any redecorating in your new office?" He looked at me as if I had two heads. "What? I'm telling you that I may be losing my new job, and you're asking me if I bought any new pillows?" "No, that's not what I'm asking," I replied. "What I'm asking is, have you hung any of the old photos and plaques that used to hang in your old office?" He said, no, he hadn't; redecorating had been the last thing on his mind. I told him it should be the first thing he did the following morning when he got into work. I told him that he needed to remember who he is, and how successful he had been in the past. He needed to start coaching himself and provide daily visual reminders that referred to his past performances and success. He was in the job for a reason, because he was good at it. And though there is a real learning curve with any new position, he needed to refocus on the confidence, ability, and determination that had gotten him to where he was. Whenever doubts arose, he needed to redirect that negative emotion and focus on positives. The next day the pictures were on the walls of his new office. And he was well on his way to working through the negative slump. If you've caught yourself spiraling down the wrong road, here are some other techniques that the article in *The Wall Street Journal* mentions to regain control and continue with your flip.

CHEAT SHEET TO BEAT NEGATIVE THINKING

- After a mistake or failure, immediately focus on a past success.
- Visualize yourself succeeding with the next sale, meeting, play, or game.
- Record and refer to your past peak performances, on video or in writing.
- List your strengths and assets and refer to the list in stressful moments.
- Turn off your mind and focus on step-by-step processes.
- Use rest or relaxation techniques such as deep breathing.
- Surround yourself with encouraging people.
- Develop rituals to focus your mind on the present moment.

- Recall the original purpose or attraction that drew you to your sport or job.
- Work with a psychologist or therapist to identify causes of performance blocks.

Each of these steps is a building process. Though you can't turn the page on your past overnight, you can take responsibility, stop blaming others, and keep it from sabotaging your success. If you practice what we've discussed, you will be well on your way. Now that you've prepared your mind to flip the script, we'll move into the next section and look at the process and strategies for executing the flip. Take a deep breath—you've completed the first part of the book, which has been about self-discovery and an understanding that no matter what the opportunities or circumstances, we need to fix ourselves and our attitudes before we can even begin to flip the script. As Lauryn Hill sang in her hit song "Doo Wop," "How you gonna win if you ain't right within?" If you've absorbed that notion, you're ready to move on to the next step.

Part Two

Navigate

The opportunity to secure ourselves against
defeat lies in our own hands, but the opportunity
of defeating the enemy is provided
by the enemy himself.

—SUN TZU

Chapter 4

The Process

Obstacles are those frightful things you see when
you take your eyes off your goal.

—HENRY FORD

AS ANY RUNNER KNOWS, the hardest part of any race is taking the
first step. The challenge lies in getting to the starting line and committing to a course of action. To successfully compete, one must train
and prepare both physically and mentally. The same is true with flipping. I can't tell you the countless times in my life that I've been staring straight ahead at a challenge, and it seemed so daunting that all I
wanted to do was crawl back into bed, pull the covers over my head,
hide, and wish it would go away. The problem is that you really can't
hide and problems don't just disappear.

As I've mentioned, I think goals and challenges are like going to
the dentist. You can keep putting them off, but eventually, as with
cavities, you're going to have to deal with them. If you wait too long
to go to the dentist or to deal with issues that are holding you back,
the pain of finally handling the problem can be twice as bad. I've
spent the first four chapters discussing how to get yourself mentally
prepared. You've reflected on the past and looked at the role you play
in determining your present reality and your future. Now I'm going
to ask you to incorporate what you've learned and begin the process
of actually flipping the script.

In the introduction I asked you to name a flip. Now that you have a better understanding of the process of flipping, has your flip changed? Or is there greater context to the original flip? Is your initial flip the primary issue or just a symptom of a greater issue that you need to tackle? I think it will be helpful to revisit the process of creating an achievable flip:

1. Clearly define your flip.
   a. Name ten situations in your life that you would like to or need to change—at work, at school, at home, in relationships, anything goes.
   b. Prioritize your list of flips: rank them from 1 to 10.
   c. Decide what exactly is entailed in achieving each flip. For example, if you want to go back and get an MBA, have you taken the GREs? When are they given? Do you have all the necessary undergraduate prerequisites? How will you pay for school? Can you work and attend school at night? And so on.
   d. Identify which flip is your number one priority.
2. Set a completion date for achieving your flip.
3. Put action behind your good intentions: stay motivated. This can be tough for anyone, so later in the book I'll discuss strategies and techniques to help you complete what you've started.

Let's get started.

NAME THAT FLIP

Though it's true that the best things in life can often come from dreaming big, it's also important to note that for dreams to come true, they need to be based in reality. It's valuable, healthy, and fun to think about all that could be, but it's equally important to think of your dreams like hot-air balloons—each must be tied with a string to reality, a weightier ballast. Without that weight, you may find yourself and your dreams floating, hopelessly lost, with no clear direction.

With that in mind, I want you to look at the piece of paper on which you've written your flips. Now that you've taken some time to reflect on the value of personal accountability, and the pitfalls of self-destructive behavior, you should have a healthy new perspective from which to view your original flip. Ask yourself, is my flip based in reality? Has it changed? Ask yourself again, what is it that I want to achieve? Is it something concrete, such as a promotion, raise, or new job? Or is it something more intangible, such as fostering better relationships with my spouse, kids, or coworkers?

There is something very empowering and real about putting your goals or aspirations on a piece of paper. Writing creates a permanent record of your thoughts. It forces you to make a commitment to an idea. In our increasingly complex world, keeping a written record is important. This is in direct contrast to the way of the ancient world. In Plato's time, for example, the written word was thought of as almost vulgar. Plato favored the spoken word—hence the rich oral tradition of Greece and other ancient civilizations—rather than the written one, saying that writing "will implant forgetfulness in their [men's] souls." Well, Plato could never have foreseen the global village we live in now, with texting, email, Facebook, and Twitter allowing every thought and action to be permanently captured and spread throughout the world via the Internet. Capturing something and transforming it into something tangible and in black and white has power and permanence. Just think, where would businesses be without capturing their company's mission and culture in writing?

Writing down your goals and your planned flips is like creating your own personal mission statement. As with business, the hard part isn't writing goals down, it's the work required to achieve them. But words without action are a waste. This is the main concept behind my approach: I combine words with action and add accountability. When you create your goals and begin to measure your progress, keeping a written record is a must. It grounds you and makes what you desire visible so that you can turn it into action and make it reality.

A flip starts out in your head as an idea, but once you write it down it becomes a plan. But the plan needs to be clear and well defined.

DEFINE YOUR FLIP CLEARLY

You can't achieve your flip if it's not clear exactly what you want to achieve. The more clearly defined the flip, the more likely your success. The less clearly defined, the harder it will be to succeed. So take some time and think hard about it. Without a clear flip you will waste time and energy, with no visible return on your hard work.

For example, "Better relationships with my coworkers" may be your flip. Though this is a solid flip, you need to ask yourself, What might a better relationship look like? Why this over any other flips? How will I judge my success? How will I determine my success? When can I complete the flip? In my experience, after you answer those questions, you often end up with a flip that is altogether different from the one you initially envisioned. Here are some steps to help you manage the process so that you choose the flip that is best for your needs, circumstances, and motivations. It may not be as easy as it seems at first glance. And for certain people, choosing the right flip is an essential cornerstone for future success. To help you with the process, I've created a flipping worksheet to help you better organize your thoughts.

FLIPPING WORKSHEET

Start by writing down all the flips that immediately come to mind; name everything you want. This is the free-thinking part, but limit them to one sentence. Come up with at least ten possible flips, and keep in mind that they can be from any aspect of your life: career, extracurricular, personal, and so on.

FLIPS

1. Career: Advance to the next level in my company.

2. Financial: Increase my take-home pay by 10 percent.

3. Education: Go for an MBA.

4. Family: Take the kids on more trips so they can experience other cultures.

5. Creative: Start a blog and write weekly posts.

6. Attitude: Adopt a more positive, can-do outlook.

7. Exercise: Run a marathon.

8. Health: Get my blood pressure down on a consistent basis.

9. Relationships: Spend more leisure time with my spouse.

10. Other: Do some kind of volunteer work.

Action: Now rank the flips into the following categories: things you would love to have or do, things you would like to have or do, and things you believe are possible to have or do. It could look something like this:

PRIORITY FLIPS

1. Career: Advance to the next level in my company.

2. Relationships: Spend more leisure time with my spouse.

3. Financial: Increase my take-home pay by 10 percent.

4. Health: Get my blood pressure down on a consistent basis.

5. Creative: Start a blog and write weekly posts.

6. Education: Go for an MBA.

7. Family: Take the kids on more trips so they can experience other cultures.

8. Attitude: Adopt a more positive, can-do outlook.

9. Exercise: Run a marathon.

10. Other: Do some kind of volunteer work.

Action: Now go back and start adding some depth to those flips. What else might be involved? Who are the players needed to succeed? Create the full script.

Let me explain why understanding how all the elements of your flip are connected is important. Recently I was working with one of my close colleagues, who believed she was ready for an internal promotion. She was smart and had worked hard over the course of several years, and the results proved her worth to the company. But her current position was largely sales-related, and though she was certainly good at her job, the promotion she sought would expand her responsibilities and include oversight and management of both sales and marketing teams.

When we sat down to talk, she was confused and frustrated. She explained to me how hard she was working and how she wanted to make this promotion happen quickly. She was eager to complete her flip. She felt she was ready for the next step in her career. In her mind she had envisioned the promotion as her flip. She had worked hard to perform well in her current position and created the currency she felt she needed to move forward. She'd thought about what she needed to achieve performancewise in her job and had delivered. In her estimation she would and should be ready for promotion. So why wasn't it happening?

We reviewed her flip and the steps she had taken. I explained to her that I felt that she hadn't dived deeply enough into her flip. She needed to add some steps and consider all of the additional stakeholders who would ultimately play a part, either directly or indirectly, in making the decision about her readiness. I said that bosses listen to all their constituents, not just you. When we explored further, I questioned whether she had won over all the marketing teams that would report to her in her newly expanded role. She hadn't considered them, as they were not directly related to her past position. "Why waste the time?" she'd thought. "They're not my boss." And though it was true that she didn't report to them, their opinions did in fact matter. She needed to add more steps to her flip because the impact of others on your flip is crucial; it's called getting stakeholders' support. You need to be aware that there may be others who can and will play a part in helping or hindering your flip.

GET STAKEHOLDER SUPPORT

The idea of getting stakeholder support is well covered in Keith Ferrazzi's book *Who's Got Your Back: The Breakthrough Program to Build Deep, Trusting Relationships That Create Success—and Won't Let You Fail,* in which he encourages readers to develop long-term, authentic relationships with those who can support them as they follow whatever path they are on or one they wish to pursue in the future. This is a symbiotic relationship, wherein the more you want to get, the more you need to give. Seth Godin has a somewhat more evolved view in his book *Linchpin: Are You Indispensable?,* according to which you should position yourself so that you are indispensable to your group. But whereas Godin applies it strictly to a professional setting, I'm confident that it would work just as well in personal endeavors. Essentially, Godin believes that every individual has the ability to contribute value to an organization in two ways: one, with bursts of creative genius during which he or she allows him- or herself to create innovative solutions where others have been unsuccessful, and two, by performing the functions that his or her company expects more and more efficiently. The less time it takes people to do their normal job because they are so adept at it, the more time they have to focus on creating value in other ways.

Godin calls his book "a personal manifesto," and it certainly reads like one. He makes the great point that if you can prove yourself indispensable by delivering value in ways outside your normal job description, you will be able to design your future. This goes back to what I talked about earlier: the more value you create and responsibility you take on, the more leverage you have in gaining support in getting whatever it is you want.

Now, considering all these things, go back and make certain you've added depth to your flip. Who else's support might you need? How can you assume more responsibility or take on roles that will enhance your worth to your company?

PRIORITY FLIPS

1. Career: Advance to the next level in my company.

IMMEDIATE MANAGER AND HIS BOSS:
- Do I have his or her support?
- Is my work visible to my boss's boss?
- Do they view me as a top performer?
- What would I need to do to become a top performer?
- Am I managing up?

CURRENT TEAM: DIRECT REPORTS, COWORKERS:
- Would others champion my promotion?
- Am I managing down?
- What do I need to get their support and respect?
- Am I an effective leader where I am?
- Have I asked my peers where they think I need help?

CLIENTS:
- What do my clients say about me to my boss?
- Do I have their support?

PARTNER:
- Is my partner on board with my promotion even if it means longer hours at work?
- Do I have my partner's support for increased travel and less free time with my family?

2. Relationships: Spend more leisure time with my spouse.

PARTNER:
- What are the things I'm interested in and the things my partner enjoys?
- Would my partner be willing to try some things I enjoy?
- What are new things we could do together?
- What day of the week allows us the most unstructured time?

KIDS:
- Do I have the kids' support to spend time with my spouse and not always as a family?
- Can I ask the kids to babysit?

3. Financial: Increase my take-home pay by 10 percent.

FAMILY:
- Is everyone on board with my working longer hours or taking on side jobs?
- What will the kids' reaction be if I can no longer coach their sports teams or carpool?

ENTREPRENEUR NETWORK:
- Have I built a network of contacts to get additional work?
- What would I need to do to build a good network?
- Who could be my first new client?

4. Health: Get my blood pressure down on a consistent basis.

HEALTH CARE PROFESSIONALS:
- Have I been to see a doctor lately?
- Has the doctor made any recommendations?

BOSS AND COLLEAGUES:
- Would my boss support my working out, either during lunch or coming in fifteen minutes late in the morning?
- Could I enlist a buddy at the office to join me in better eating habits at lunch?

FAMILY:
- Is everyone supportive of my new health plan?
- Will my spouse walk the dog so I can work out before work?
- How could we all change our diets?
- What exercise could we do as a family?

Action: Once you've mapped out the additional aspects of your flip, reread your original list. Which is the one that stands out the most? Which is most meaningful to you? This is the Alpha Flip, and it is the one you need to start with. The Alpha Flip reflects where your passion lies— and what you are most passionate about is what you will work hardest to complete.

 Flip Tip: Narrow down your flips to the most important to you; this is the Alpha Flip.

GIVE YOUR FLIP A COMPLETION DATE

You have now figured out your flip! Excited? I hope so. You are on your way. Once you have named your flip, the question you need to ask yourself is "When do I want to accomplish this?" "Someday" is not the right answer. An open-ended delivery date just doesn't work; adhering to a realistic but pressure-related timetable does. Without the pressure of a deadline, as we all know, nothing gets accomplished.

In my own experience, time and pressure are major motivators. Take writing this book, for instance. And yes, this book was a flip for me. I must tell you, at first the idea of writing a book seemed simple. How hard could it be? I thought. Well, I was wrong. Very hard, it turns out. I needed to become very focused with my time. For me, writing a two-hundred-plus-page book while holding down a high-intensity full-time job, not to mention juggling the responsibilities that come along with raising my three kids, represented a dramatic change in my life. I needed not only to become very organized but also to garner my stakeholders' support. Writing this book has meant spending basically every weekend for the past year in front of a computer—writing and rewriting. Time management has been essential to the process. In the end, it has been completely worth it. This book is such an important flip for me; it is an opportunity to share my twenty years of experience, techniques, and tactics to provide hope for all those who think they can't change their current circumstances and achieve their goals. I'm happy now, but when I started the process I had no idea of exactly how the process worked and how long the book would take to write. That may be the case for you as well. To share a bit of the background on my flip, when pitching the idea, I worked hard with the help of my talented agents, Jan Miller and Shannon Marven of Dupree Miller & Associates, to secure a book deal, but what happened after the contract was signed was completely foreign to me. A publisher—in my case, Free Press—gives an author essentially one year to write and submit the final manuscript. As I had never written a book before, the process seemed daunting, particularly because of the time frame the publisher proposed. It was just too long. I never think that a lot of time is a good thing. I feared that I might lose interest or energy and move on to something else, another flip. To do it right, flipping takes focus. So, to help manage time, I actually shortened the time period that was proposed to me and instead gave myself a six-month window rather than the year to complete the majority of the text. As I write this today, I am halfway through, with three months to go on my schedule. (Later P.S.: I'm glad I gave myself that shorter writing schedule because in the end I needed all the time. What I didn't account for was editorial copy changes, which were painfully extensive. I am now completing the final polish on the book with only two weeks till deadline.)

Try to be honest with yourself when you set a completion date. Don't give yourself all the time in the world to accomplish your flip—add a bit of pressure to your passion! The best flip in the world will mean nothing if you haven't created a realistic timetable for completion. If this is your first flip, remember that you will get better at it, and with time you'll learn to map out a realistic approach.

 Flip Tip: Create a realistic but pressure-related timetable for your flip.

STAY S.M.A.R.T.

My approach to naming your flip and setting goals is rooted in one of the earliest, yet most time-tested, approaches to goal setting. Edwin Locke was one of the pioneers in management theory, and his theory of goal setting has most likely influenced every modern approach.

In the late 1960s Locke created the approach known as "management by objectives," which is pretty commonly used today. If you're not familiar with it, essentially this means that managers give employees a specific set of goals designed to increase their motivation and performance. Interestingly, Locke found that the more challenging the goal, the better the employee performed. Locke's thinking became the foundation of the field of organizational psychology.

Locke's S.M.A.R.T. method describes effective goal setting as being:

- **S**pecific
- **M**easurable
- **A**ttainable
- **R**elevant
- **T**ime-bound

Ask yourself, is your flip S.M.A.R.T.? Recently Locke updated his thinking with a coauthor, Gary P. Latham, adapting goal setting to the modern business world. In an article in *The American Psychologist,* Locke and Latham said that setting the right goals can impact performance because goals focus attention toward goal-relevant activities and away from goal-irrelevant activities. For example, if your goal is to be promoted at work, over the next six months goal-relevant activities may include coming into the office early every day and being the last to leave. That clearly demonstrates your commitment to the company. Goal-irrelevant activity may include organizing the office softball team. That work-related activity does not move you closer to achieving your goal. When thinking about your flip, consider the following:

1. "Goals serve as an energizer; higher goals will induce greater effort, while low goals induce lesser effort. Basically, the harder the goal, the more it can energize. The easier the goal, the less value and effort you will put into it.
2. Goals affect persistence; constraints with regard to resources will affect work pace.
3. Goals activate cognitive knowledge and strategies, which allows employees to cope with the situation at hand."

Locke has been researching and honing his method for the last forty years and writing about it in books, journals, and magazines. Let's face it, the reason he is so trusted is that it works.

In addition to what we can learn from business books, let's consider for a moment what we can learn from individuals outside the office. Dedicating yourself to achieving your goals and performing at high levels while you do it are the hallmarks of professional athletes. Over the years I've adapted some of athletes' techniques to business and found that they can serve you well by providing some very useful advice about how to rise above distractions and perform well under pressure.

The sports psychologist Don Greene has worked with everyone from Grand Prix racers to Olympic athletes, specializing in how to help them maintain a high level of performance under pressure. In his book *Fight Your Fear and Win: Seven Skills for Performing Your Best Under Pressure—at Work, in Sports, on Stage,* Greene identifies seven critical qualities you need to stay victorious in challenging situations. They are determination, energy, perspective, courage, focus, poise, and resilience. They are easy to name but not so easy to achieve. In the next sections, I'll tell you how you can find the determination and mental discipline to achieve your flip. Now that you have the courage to name your flip, we'll cover how you can stay focused and resist traps while keeping your poise. Like all things that last, it starts with a commitment.

COMMIT TO THE FLIP

To win, we need to keep our determination, energy, perspective, and focus strong. This isn't always easy in our busy world. Most of us differ from professional athletes in that yes, we want to achieve our flips, but most likely we have full-time jobs and busy personal lives, and staying singularly focused can be hard. Flipping takes practice and discipline—so, as suggested above, create a manageable and specific timetable to measure your success. Take into consideration anything that may cause a delay. If you're not happy with your progress, examine why you haven't achieved the flip already. Do you have any conscious or unconscious habits that are blocking your way? Why is it so easy to say "I'll commit" but so hard to do? One main reason is that after years of forming bad habits, staying focused is tough.

BREAK BAD HABITS

To flip you need to break your bad habits. Plain and simple, habitual behavior and flipping are not friends. Let me explain why. When you do something for a long period of time, it becomes a habit. Some habits may be good, such as going to bed early, brushing your teeth, and looking both ways before you cross the street. But when it comes to business and achieving your flips, you need to break the mold—and the behaviors you do robotically are the ones that are keeping you stuck in your current situation. You need to create new, positive patterns of behavior. Habits that keep you from thinking "outside the box" can be deadly—because they are limiting and bad for your career. Why? They limit your openness to new ideas. They limit your receptivity to others' ideas and input. And at their worst they control you, keeping your behavior stuck in familiar patterns.

Want to see how unaware many of us are that we even have habitual behaviors? To illustrate this point, I'll start by asking you to fold your arms. Go ahead, cross them. Good? All right, now I want you to fold them the other way, with the arm that was on the bottom now on the top. It's tough, right?

The reason is that you've probably crossed your arms a certain way for years, your entire life, even. It feels comfortable. It's a simple habit. But when I ask you to change even a simple habit such as crossing your arms, it feels uncomfortable and awkward. Our bodies don't respond because we always go back to what we know, where we are most comfortable. Hopefully you can now see how limiting habitual behavior can be in business and in your personal life if your habits are not objective, healthy, and proactive. Habits are hard to change but not impossible. They can be changed if you know how to do it. How do you change your habits? It starts by finding out what motivates you. This is the first step in showing bad habits the door.

LEARN WHAT MOTIVATES YOU

Over the course of history, theories about how to motivate people have evolved and changed as the workplace's needs have shifted dramatically—from the demands put on workers during the Industrial Revolution to the different sets of challenges faced by people in modern corporations. I'll quickly summarize the two main approaches to motivation that are most prevalent and then discuss how I think you can adapt the model and make it work for you.

1. Carrot and the Stick: This theory was developed by the mechanical engineer Frederick Taylor in the early 1900s. According to this theory, average people didn't like working and would avoid it if at all possible. Because of their natural dislike of work, employers needed to coerce them to get them to put in any kind of adequate effort. This is the carrot-and-stick approach. I bet everyone is familiar with this idea: you reward good behavior and punish bad behavior. This type of motivation has been adapted a million ways. I've even seen it done by taking the carrots away; I could call this the starvation approach. I once knew a very senior-level executive who advised his direct reports that they were to keep their staffs "afraid and hungry." I don't really think you will get the best out of your people or yourself with this type of approach. But you need to ask yourself, are you a carrot person? Do you seek rewards for your good behavior? Or are you a Theory Y person?

2. Theory X & Y, developed by Douglas McGregor at MIT in the 1960s, holds that people do, in fact, want to be active participants in their job, respond to being treated with dignity (rather than being tempted with some reward), and are capable of managing themselves; that is, they are self-directed. If you are this type of person, you probably don't need to make yourself run an extra mile to give yourself permission to have a second piece of pie. Regardless of whether you conform to Theory X or Theory Y, understanding what motivates you is an important part of staying focused on achieving your flip.

The connection that has to be made in reviewing all this organizational and philosophical theory is that you must activate your desire to achieve your end goal. Whether it is motivating a team or motivating yourself, you have to really want to achieve the goal. And you need to understand the reasons why. It makes no difference whether the goal is a 30 percent increase in productivity in the factory or a 30 percent decline in your waistline. Goals need to be clearly defined and named in a way that makes it obvious how desirable they are to you.

• • •

Over the past twenty years, having led teams and motivated hundreds of people, I've boiled down what I feel are consistent primary motivations into three behavioral types:

1. **The Gold Star Seeker: Recognition and reward**

     This type of motivation occurs when individuals are focused on "acquisition," or a gold star. This motivation comes from the desire for more money, power, recognition, or influence. Often in this scenario individuals feel as though they are moving *toward* something. There is a "thing" in a person's mind that he or she seeks to acquire, and it is that quest which keeps him or her motivated. Is your flip an acquisition?

2. **The Breaking Point: Desire for happiness**

     This type of motivation is usually associated with unhappy or unhealthy situations. It occurs when an individual grows tired of a situation and wants to find renewed happiness or control. He or she has hit a breaking point and is motivated to change. Breaking Point motivation comes from the desire to move *away from an unhealthy situation. Is your flip about gaining happiness?*

3. **The Transitional: Life changes**

     Individuals who are motivated to make a change in this

scenario are truly neutrals. They are motivated by indirect circumstances or choices: a new marriage, a baby on the way, job relocation, retirement, divorce. Their motivation comes with a specific event and timetable. Is your flip about transition?

Whatever your essential motivation, you are going to need to find ways to create daily motivational support. If you are a Gold Star Seeker, I suggest printing out on your printer a business card with your "new title" and placing it on the refrigerator, or hanging a picture of your dream house or vacation on your cube wall. If you are a Breaking Point who is trying to lose weight, try placing a photo of a model in a bathing suit over your cookie jar. Or what about writing yourself a love letter, telling yourself all the wonderful things you like about yourself? Positive affirmations can be a powerful tool in staying motivated. A few years back my flip was a breaking point. I was tired of feeling out of shape. So I made my flip to complete a local triathlon. Throughout the process, whenever I felt my motivations were slipping, as when it was too cold outside or I had already lost five pounds and thought to myself, "Wasn't that good enough?"—I used affirmations to stay focused. Every morning when I got into the freezing pool and swam my laps, I would repeat to myself over and over three positive affirmations: "You are strong," "You don't quit," "You can do this." What is the message you'd like to tell yourself? Trust me: though it may sound a bit cheesy, it works. Finally, if you are a pregnant Transitional and looking for daily motivation, what's more powerful than seeing your baby's sonogram on the refrigerator? That's enough motivation to do everything from eating right to decorating the baby's room.

BREAK IT DOWN

After reading the above, ask yourself, What motivates me? Is it built into your flip already? If you're looking to advance in your career and a promotion is your flip, what is driving you to achieve this, now that it's going to mean you will have to commit to many long workdays and weekends? Is it the money? That's okay; money is a major motivator in life and business. But if that is your answer, you need to take it a step further to motivate yourself and break it down. Think about what you will use the money for. Is it to pay for your kid's college tuition or to buy a new car or your own home? Again, you need daily motivation. So put a picture of the college campus up in your cube or have the car as a screen saver on your computer. I really believe in the power of the visual. Having a physical incarnation of your goal—a picture, a message, a poem, whatever—in front of you every day really helps you to stay focused and motivated. No flip is going to be achieved without hard work, sacrifice, and self-discipline, but visualizing the end result this way can work wonders.

In addition to motivating yourself through visualization, you should also craft questions that really get at the heart of why you want to make a certain flip. For example: Why do you want an MBA? It will definitely pay off in future jobs—and the degree does make you a desirable hire. Or is it because you ultimately want to strike out on your own and create your own company? That business schooling will certainly improve your chances of success. Here is a list of the kinds of questions that work best in terms of getting to the right answer:

What are you looking to flip?
What will happen when you achieve your flip?
What are several benefits of your flip?
How can your flip increase your overall happiness and sense of
    self-worth?

The answers to these questions are your motivators, and you need to keep them at the top of your mind. Just as you need to figure out which behaviors are keeping you from achieving your goals, you need to be sure you're feeding what drives you. There are no wrong answers; it doesn't matter whether your motives are philanthropic or mercenary. Avoid the traps discussed previously; then figure out what your true motivation is and feed it.

 Flip Tip: Feed your flip: know what motivates you, and keep it front and center.

By now you know what your flip is and you've figured out ways to keep putting one foot in front of the other to achieve it. But what about when things get tough? How do you make the hard choices? That is, how do you actually follow through on taking actions to complete achieving your flip in spite of the challenges that come into play? That is the subject of the next chapter.

Chapter 5

The Right Thing and
the Hard Thing

Wisdom is knowing what to do next; virtue is doing it.

—DAVID STARR JORDAN, PEACE ACTIVIST

AS THE SAYING GOES, the right thing and the hard thing are often the same thing. This is such a fundamentally important principle to understand in the process of activating your script that I want to spend an entire chapter talking about it. Doing the right thing is so hard because it usually takes much more work, determination, willpower, and self-control than you'd expect. Believe me, I know. Like so many others, I am confronted with this dilemma on a daily basis. In fact, as I'm sitting here writing this chapter, I'm on an American Airlines flight back to New York from the men's fashion shows in Milan, Italy. Milan during fashion week has its own subculture. It's a place where abnormally young, abnormally tall, and abnormally fit people wear abnormally expensive clothes and somehow become the norm. I am none of the above. And after a week of watching them, it was I who wound up feeling abnormal.

As all the frenzy of fashion week races around the back of my mind, the flight attendant is just circling me for the third time with the breadbasket. She has a big smile on her face as she stands in front of me with that warm fragrant smell of airline fresh-ish bread—she can sense that I *want* that bread. I should disclose that bread or any bakery-type food is a major weakness of mine. There are a million tough choices and daily temptations that keep us from sticking to our goals. Those challenges are the proverbial forks in the road that we face every day in our business and personal lives. Maybe for you it's not fighting off the breadbasket; maybe it's that you haven't completed an assignment that has to be turned in, but it's Friday and the gang from the office is ready to go out for drinks. Whatever it may be, making good choices is all about getting ourselves to think about the end result and stay focused on the goal. Beating temptations and distractions takes an incredible amount of self-control and also a harsh reality check. In his book *The 7 Habits of Highly Effective People,* Stephen R. Covey advises readers to think about the end result. Another way to focus on your goals is to consider how you want people to remember you. Keep this in mind as you go about your professional and personal lives; base your decisions and actions on what you want that final perception to be. Are you a person whom everyone trusts and knows will always follow through on his commitments? Getting this kind of external perspective often helps, but in my opinion what's more motivating than the judgments of others is self-judgment. Think about doing things that you are proud of and value. When you look in the mirror, are you proud of the person you see there? When you are, there is no better feeling in the world—and it doesn't cost a dime.

To get back to the reality check I mentioned earlier: as I see it, there is no such thing as overnight success, in business or in anything else. Behind every success story are long hours of self-sacrifice and hard work. Everything has a price—either it's monetary time-related, or it comes from your soul. Success may look easy to those on the outside, but appearances are often deceiving. I remember a friend of mine, Kurt, who was what in New York society circles is called a "walker." This is an old-school term for gay men who hang with "fabulous" socialites. Typically the women are supersocial and love to go out most nights, attending society functions and benefits. Often their husbands are uninterested and too focused on their work to want to accompany them. The women don't want to attend the functions alone, so they take their gay best friends, who wind up being their "walkers." When friends would get together with Kurt, they would rave about how incredible life must be for those women. Some would be envious of the women's lives for what they perceived as a life of ease full of money, luxury, and fun parties. Of course, many people might think this lifestyle to be ideal and would be jealous of those women. But Kurt often told a different story. He would say with complete seriousness, "Whenever anyone marries for money, trust me, they always wind up earning it." Meaning that from the outside, it's impossible to know what those women have to put up with behind closed doors. And whether you are a socialite or a social worker, there are no shortcuts in life. Success takes work.

 Flip Tip: Never judge your "insides" by someone else's "outsides."

Nowhere have I seen this lesson more evident than in Hollywood. I advise people not to believe any celebrities who tell you they owe their appearance to "good genes," "walking everywhere," or "chasing after their children." I can honestly tell you that this is baloney. I have never met an actor, celebrity, or sports star who looked good who wasn't fanatical about his or her appearance, health, and body. Many are constantly on a "cleansing" diet or eat only the healthiest fat-free, gluten-free, pesticide-free, organic whatever. And good for them, it works, and they look amazing and fit. But we should not let their relaxed attitudes—or indeed anyone who says change isn't difficult— fool us into believing that there's an easy road or shortcut to success.

The same holds true in business. If you want to advance in your career, get a better compensation package, and gain the attention of management, you have to put in the hard work. That means that you have to not only meet but also exceed expectations. Keep the end result—your goals—at the forefront of your mind, and be sure to implement some of the motivational tactics I mentioned earlier. In the end you gotta stick with it; continuity works best. To illustrate my point, I'll tell you about a sales call I made years ago that has always stuck with me. The call was to a cosmetics company, and it had a profound impact on my personal and professional views of achieving results and particularly of "doing the right thing."

WHAT DO HAVING CLEAR SKIN AND FLIPPING HAVE IN COMMON?

Many years ago I was on the West Coast for a sales call to a large and very successful cosmetics company. After meeting with a few executives I was offered the opportunity to visit their factory and see the scientific processes behind the creation of their beauty products. The facilities were impressive and produced effective and commercially successful products. During the tour I had the opportunity to chat with one of the company's lab chemists, who specialized in creating the company's acne medications. We talked briefly, and I inquired about what separated its products from those of its competitors. He started out by saying that the basic ingredients of all acne medicines are pretty much the same; sure, one may use a slightly different formula, but for all intents and purposes they all use salicylic acid as the main component. In his opinion, though, what made for a successful acne product wasn't just the ingredients but the customer's commitment to maintaining a proper application regimen. Basically, those who followed the routine rigorously obtained the best results. The same is true in business: you can achieve the best results by consistency. Doing something every day that gets you closer to your flip.

When you're working on a flip, you must remember that results take time and that you must commit to daily success. To that end, some techniques that I have found work well in building daily success are:

1. Add something new every day. Try to find one thing every day from your flip that you felt you learned from—good, bad, whatever—write it down in a notebook, and use it to propel yourself forward. It is incredible what will accumulate over time.

2. Just do it. As Nike's ad campaign put it, nothing produces results better than doing, so do what needs to be done

today: set up that meeting, book that trip, call and apologize. Do something daily that takes you closer to achieving your flip.

3. Listen twice as much as you talk. Practice the art of listening; you will be amazed at what you learn from people, and how it can help you in achieving your flip, when you keep your mouth closed.

4. Don't waste time. Time management is crucial. Have a daily plan for what you want to accomplish—and make sure to build in time for yourself, including time for gym, friends, and family.

5. Define success daily. Think to yourself in the morning, "Today would be a good day if I accomplished _____." Then do it. Small victories build confidence and keep your motivation high.

When you combine all these behaviors, doing the right thing and taking action, you will be on your way to a successful flip.

ACTIONS MUST FOLLOW WORDS

If your goal at work is to be promoted a level, it stands to reason that you need to put in some extra effort. No clocking out after an eight-hour day or going to happy hour on Thursday evening with your buddies and writing off having a productive Friday. If you're committed to the idea of being promoted, your actions have to follow suit. If you know that staying out late during the week hurts your performance at work, the answer is really quite simple: wait until Friday night! It always amazes me when people complain about not having their boss's support or attention when they don't give 110 percent of themselves. They feel as though other people are catching all the breaks. But here's a thought: come in early, stay late, and volunteer for assignments that take you out of your job function. It's called *taking the initiative; you need to show your boss that side of you. Just as in golf, it's all about the follow-through.*

Why is this often so hard to do? Is it something we are born with? Are some of us just better at following through? How can we learn to follow through on the goals we set? How can a marshmallow demonstrate how we can learn to follow through? Read on.

THE MARSHMALLOW TEST

On April 21, 2010, I heard a fascinating report on CBS News that proclaimed, "Studies show that kids who can force themselves to wait for greater rewards tend to go on to better academic and personal lives." The experiment upon which the 2010 study was based was called the "marshmallow experiment." Originally conducted by Walter Mischel at Stanford University in the 1960s, it had recently been conducted again. The setup of the test was simple: four-year-old children were individually given one marshmallow and promised a second one on the condition that they wait several minutes before eating the first one.

Some children were able to wait, while others could not. The researchers then followed the progress of each child into adolescence and saw that those with the ability to wait were better adjusted and more dependable (this was determined based on surveys of their parents and teachers) and scored significantly higher on the SATs. They continued to follow the participants for more than thirty years and concluded that those who practiced the greatest amount of self-control and willpower achieved at the highest levels. The studies have been so successful that they still continue today. Researchers consistently find that the kids who could force themselves to wait tend to have better lives and relationships. They've also averaged a whopping 210 points higher on the SATs than the kids who could not hold off.

This shows that success or flipping the script isn't based on intelligence; rather, it's based on our ability to manage ourselves and control our urges. Mischel argued that intelligence is largely at the mercy of self-control. He concludes that even the brightest kids in the class still need to do homework. About his original experiment, he commented, "What we're really measuring with the marshmallows isn't willpower or self-control. It's much more important than that; this task forces kids to find a way to make the situation work for them. They want the second marshmallow, but how can they get it? We can't control the world, but we can control how we think about it."

In their book *Switch: How to Change Things When Change Is Hard,* the Heath brothers, Chip and Dan, talk about similar research studies in which *self-control* was the "rider" and *uninhibited behavior,* "the elephant." The more the rider had to do to control the elephant early on, the more tired the rider became. When you apply that metaphor to human behavior, it means that the more you have to do to control yourself early in the process of doing something—a diet, for instance—the harder it is to sustain your self-discipline. You're simply worn out by the task's demands in the beginning. What's important to remember is that it's just the beginning when you're trying to change behavior. It gets easier as you go along, and, as when training a muscle, the more you work on it, the stronger it gets. This is what flipping is all about: understanding that we have the ability to manage how we respond to situations. The more we do it, the easier it becomes. What if you don't have natural self-control or willpower? How can you get it? How can you keep your rider in charge of the elephant? I'll offer some exercises here to help you as you try to gain or master self-control.

PLAYING MIND GAMES CAN INCREASE YOUR WILLPOWER

You might be wondering if playing mind games can really help you achieve your goals and flip your script. I say yes, it can. Mischel's research also uncovered a shortcut for learning delayed gratification skills. He and his colleagues used simple mental tricks to help the children. They pretended that the marshmallow in front of them was not real, only a picture. This mental exercise allowed for more of the children who had eaten the marshmallow the first time around to control their behavior and wait several minutes for the reward of two marshmallows. In business and life, using tricks like this can make it easier to think about the steps you need to take in flipping your script. For example, if your flip is improving your relationship with a difficult boss, what if every time you went in to see him or her, you thought about how he or she might be struggling with some major issues in his or her personal life? Would that affect how you dealt with that person? Although you're pretending in this case, this practice can be valuable; it could make you more understanding or compassionate. Remember, your goal is not to change anyone else or the world. Your intention is to focus on managing yourself and the goals you are working toward. I have to admit that playing mind games is a trick I use all the time, especially when work is starting to overwhelm me and there is just too much to do. When I get overwhelmed, I start to lose focus, and when that happens, nothing gets accomplished.

So to save myself, I pretend that there is nothing else to do but one task. And when I finish that I will be all done. I force myself to forget about everything else around me. I just think: all that I have to do is complete this one task. It is a way of distracting yourself from whatever overwhelms you that allows you to make progress incrementally. And it works. Small victories are important.

 Flip Tip: To increase your focus, tell yourself that you need to accomplish only one thing and forget everything else. When that is completed, go on to the next thing, apply the same thinking, and so on.

Another great way to keep your focus is to adopt the practice of "mindfulness," or being in the moment. This technique stems from Buddhism but is useful for people from all cultures and backgrounds and can be put to a variety of purposes, including business situations. Mindfulness requires you to do one thing: focus on what it is you're doing at that exact moment and "be present" in whatever it is you're involved with. So if you're watching a movie with your spouse, don't be thinking about what the boss said to you yesterday or the trip you're planning next month; really take the time to fully experience the time with your partner. The same holds true whether you're doing something really simple, such as eating a sandwich, or more complex, such as reviewing a contract. Essentially, it's the idea of being in the moment and doing whatever it is you are doing and nothing else.

It sounds kind of simple, but I will tell you that it is both hard to do and very effective in breaking the distraction habit. Remember the exercise where I asked you to fold your arms in the opposite direction from the usual? It's the same kind of thing. You actually have to focus on focusing! When you catch your mind wandering, bring it back to the task at hand. It's something you will need to practice, but trust me, it is a great way of developing mental discipline.

Here is another outside-the-office, personal-life example of how you can keep yourself from becoming distracted or falling into habits that keep you from your flip.

No Cell Phone Service

I have a good friend who always seems to choose the wrong guy. This is a common story. She is overly generous and selfless. She dated a couple of guys and in almost every instance the fellow was a jerk and wound up taking advantage of her kindness and the situation. Now, I'm certainly biased toward my friend, but I could see that all of this was making her unhappy, so I decided she needed some tough love to help her flip the script. We arranged to meet for lunch, and when I sat down with her, we talked about her predicament. She explained that although she had been dating the current guy for nine months, she rationally understood that the relationship wasn't healthy, but she felt stuck. Over and over, she would try to get up the strength to break up with him, but eventually she would always weaken and call him. She repeated the pattern over and over again, seemingly helpless to save herself from herself.

I told her to stop thinking about all the long-term things that were nagging at her, such as "Where is my life going?" and "What if I end up alone?"—all the issues that played into making her weak after a few days of resisting and led her to grab the phone. I told her, "Look, taking control can be simpler than you think." I continued,

"If there was no phone, you would not be able to call him. And once you were broken up, it would be over once and for all." She looked at me as if I were crazy. "But there are phones everywhere," she said. "Well, do you use phones *everywhere*?" I inquired. "No," she said. I went on to explain, "Right, you just use your cell phone, one phone. So you only have one problem, your cell phone."

I know it may seem as though I am simplifying the issues here. And if you feel that way, you're right; I am. Sometimes change can be simple. That's the trick to forgetting all the noise and boiling things down to one controllable issue. What I asked my friend to do was to try breaking up with her boyfriend yet again, but this time to imagine that she'd lost her cell phone. Whenever she thought about calling, she would tell herself that the phone was nowhere to be found. I also advised her that if she was feeling particularly weak, she should actually hide the phone somewhere in her apartment. I know that sounds crazy, and you would think that if she was the one hiding it, she'd know where to find it, but you have to remember that she wanted to make a change—she herself was tired of the roller coaster, so her will to trick herself could be surprisingly strong if she allowed it to be.

Motivation to make a change is key, because when we *want* something we can convince ourselves of anything. You know it's true, right? We do it all the time when pursuing unhealthy things. I consider this kind of approach deceiving ourselves for healthy gains. This technique is designed to trick your mind to help you through a moment of weakness and eventually accomplish your goals. And in the process of flipping, moments of weakness will come. It's how you deal with them that matters. Often the walls we hit are just momentary weak spots and are surmountable. If we can just get over them, we become stronger and so much closer to flipping our scripts.

Back to the story about my friend and her breakup. Two weeks after I told her to try getting rid of her cell phone, we met again. She had tried my advice, and, as wacky as it sounded, it had worked! She'd broken up with the bad boyfriend, and the first day or two had been tough. She'd had to fight wanting to go back to the comfort of familiar patterns, but because she'd convinced herself that her cell phone battery had died, she'd actually avoided using the phone the entire weekend, instead going out with friends and keeping herself busy.

When the weekend ended, she had made it without calling him. It was an empowering victory for her and gave her the confidence she needed to end the cycle. A week passed, and then the unexpected happened. On a Monday morning, the bad boyfriend called her. When you break old patterns, you have to be prepared for new ones to emerge. He had never called her after a breakup. It had always been she who had pursued him. But now she had changed the pattern. And when she behaved in an unexpected way, he also did something entirely new: he apologized. It felt good for her to hear him say he was sorry and that he missed her, but it was too late, she was different. She was tired of the endless circle of insecurity and lack of attention. She didn't want to go back to him. She was finally done. Seeing new patterns arise in your life is one of the most exciting parts of flipping.

As a happy footnote to this true story, six weeks later my friend met a new guy when she was out with her girlfriends. She took her newfound confidence into this new relationship, and wouldn't you know, they fell in love, married a year and a half later, and now have two beautiful children. See how much your life can change for the better when you break old habits? So how can you actually start to take the steps that will get you to your goals? To get to that answer, ask the question, "How do you eat an elephant?" The answer is "Bite by bite."

 Flip Tip: Change can be simple; boil things down to one controllable issue at a time.

EATING THE ELEPHANT BITE BY BITE

I think the secret of accomplishing any of your goals is to create a plan and set a course of action. But that's only half the battle. The second half is creating the individual steps to achieve your goals and sticking to them.

To do this I use a process that I call the *elephant process,* the reason being that when you look at any flip in totality it can seem big, scary, and unachievable. As we discovered earlier in the book, when we get scared we see all the things that won't work and how things can go wrong. We feel overwhelmed, and many times we quit before we ever get started. The elephant process is simple. It allows you to break down your flip into ten smaller steps. When you follow this process, all you have to worry about at any given time is the one small step that's right in front of you.

Turning the elephant metaphor around, we should also consider the Heaths' concept and ask ourselves, how do you train an elephant? The Heaths learned that animal trainers got their subjects—large and small—to learn certain behaviors step by small step, with lots of reinforcement along the way—just as we're trying to do here. In this process, small victories are celebrated and confidence grows—and the desired result is achieved.

I'd like you to take out the piece of paper on which you wrote your flip and write down ten steps that you need to accomplish to achieve it. Order them from one to ten, creating a chronological order. For example, if your flip is to graduate from college, you must first graduate from high school. If your flip is to lose twenty pounds, you must first lose one pound. If your flip is to write ten chapters, you must start with chapter 1.

Creating smaller, achievable goals takes the pressure off achieving the larger goal. For example, in my own current flip—writing this book—I have made each chapter an elephant bite. I have ten of them. So I don't worry about the entire book and when I will finish it on a daily basis. I don't even think about it. The book is my Alpha Flip. All I think about is each chapter. I work on finishing one chapter at a time. And every month I come closer to the main goal. You can do the same thing.

Let's take a look at the flip from the worksheet in chapter 4 that we identified as the number one priority of ten possible choices: to advance to the next level in your company. What would the steps toward achieving that look like in a worksheet? Maybe something like this:

CAREER FLIP

ADVANCE TO THE NEXT LEVEL IN MY COMPANY
ELEPHANT BITES

1. Get noticed: Be sure to offer at least one idea or comment in each meeting.

2. Create a support system: Take the time to have lunch or chat with members outside of my immediate team who are well thought of in the company—i.e., expand my circle of influence.

3. Show enthusiasm: Volunteer for assignments by the boss that are up for grabs.

4. Stand out to management: Become involved with issues and initiatives that are important to senior management.

5. Demonstrate potential: Exceed the goals in my job description— go above and beyond what's expected of me.

You'll find that with every elephant bite you achieve, your confidence rises. You feel stronger. You can see results, and that produces a motivation that is critical to committing to your flip for as long as it takes. We talked about motivation in the last chapter, and I gave you some advice about tying what drives you to the actual flip. Having that end result in mind is certainly a good motivator, but when you hit a wall, remember: this is something that is very important to you. As I said earlier, you need to be sure that whatever your flip is, it's something you really want. Next, build in reinforcing moments as you work through the process of flipping: celebrate the small victories with each bite of the elephant. These should be small rewards that you give yourself, such as a new lipstick or premium golf balls, or maybe fresh flowers or that long-promised massage. You need to learn to thank yourself for your own hard work. Think in advance: what would you like as a reward for each small goal achieved? I have my own system of self-rewards. Each time I accomplished another bite of my elephant goal I treated myself to the movies, by myself, indulging my private love for bad horror flicks or cheesy teen fare. There is something about sitting in a dark theater with a large Diet Coke and popcorn that makes me feel as though I am on vacation, if only for two hours. While at the movies I get lost in the story and think about nothing else. That is my reward, and I consider the movies my mental message. I come out two hours later, my mind rested and clear. Whether your reward is the movies or the driving range, having one in mind helps you stay motivated, and you can do it guilt free because you've earned it. Then you can enjoy the confidence that comes along with those personal successes—and use that feeling to achieve your next elephant bite.

ANY PLAN IS BETTER THAN NO PLAN

The last and most important piece of advice I can offer in terms of planning is to give yourself a break. Act like your own best friend, and give yourself the advice that you would give others. Be flexible, and realize that your plan is a work in progress. Plans may change. New opportunities and challenges may arise. But be content in the knowledge that you actually have a plan—and that any plan is better than no plan.

With a plan in place, you'll be encouraged to see your progress moving from one elephant bite to the next. That's an important aspect of keeping the momentum going. So, every day, take a moment to ask yourself if you are closer to your immediate goal. Are you better today than you were yesterday or the day before that or when you first identified your Alpha Flip? Give yourself mini–performance reviews, but keep them positive. Consider how you're moving forward, but don't beat yourself up for hitting snags along the way.

In the example I used above about advancing to the next level in your career, a common snag could be investing time in building your support system only to have a key member that you have won over relocate, forcing you to start all over with a new person. But don't worry; stay focused. Practitioners of positive psychology will tell you that when bad times hit or obstacles get in your way, you need to rethink the situation and find the hidden benefits, which just means you have to try to find the good in what has happened so far. A hidden benefit is something positive that you can take from a situation that you hadn't considered when you started the flip. Turn the experience inside out, and try to see where it may take you. Don't focus too long on the dangers or downside brought on by the event. Get past that and figure out what your next steps will be. What opportunities can you find in the new situation? Step goals, techniques to keep distractions and bad habits from hurting your momentum, and a positive attitude are the essential parts of getting on your way to achieving your flip.

Part Three

How you respond to the challenge in the second
half will determine what you become after the game,
whether you are a winner or a loser.

—LOU HOLTZ

Chapter 6

Strategic Anger and Other Offensive Moves

We boil at different degrees.

—RALPH WALDO EMERSON

OVER THE PAST SIX CHAPTERS I've focused all of the discussion inward—and I'm sure you've done a lot of great work in that direction. I've talked about how to get your head into the right place, and you've gone through the process of thinking about your goals as they relate to your own challenges and limitations. In all, you've done the internal mental homework and worked through the steps necessary to begin flipping the script. But up until now most of your work and insight have not addressed the issue of external pressures and influences that can trip you up and threaten a flip.

Much of what's been discussed in the previous chapters centered on self-reflection and understanding personal fears and motivations while creating tools for effectively managing them. Essentially, if this were a football team, we would have created a winning defense. But the world is not perfect, and everyone in it won't bend to our desires and goals just because that's what we want. It's important to understand that there will be opposition to your success from time to time. There are many factors and reasons why someone either at work or in your family will feel threatened by your new confidence and script change. In the end, you can't make people behave differently; all you can do is manage yourself. We must nevertheless be prepared for some opposition—large and small—from those around us. This opposition can be felt either directly or indirectly. So if you want to flip the script successfully, not only do you need a good defense, sometimes you also need a killer offense. In this chapter I will share some of the most effective offensive tools that I have applied or encountered in my personal and business life. Time tested and simple, these tools will help you overcome opposition and manipulation and allow you to take direct control of your flip. Specifically, I'll show you how you can harness the power of strategic anger, learn how to speak your audience's language, and assume the presence of a leader. However, before we get into how these techniques are used, you have to adopt the attitude of a winner by being a champion for yourself and putting your needs and wants ahead of others.

DON'T TAKE A SUPPORTING ROLE IN YOUR OWN LIFE STORY

Many of us, who were raised to be polite, to always listen, to be respectful of our elders or superiors—the boss, the grandparents, whoever—may find the offensive tools covered in this chapter a bit uncomfortable—at first. The reason they may make you feel uncomfortable is that we are trained at a young age to wait our turn, play by the rules, get into line, be nice, and think of others first. The techniques discussed in this chapter will require you to become your own advocate, put yourself at the front of the line, and think about your own best interests and not what benefits everyone else. It will require you to focus on what benefits *you*.

Over the years, as I've taught many sales and marketing organizations how to behave offensively—to put their interests first—I have literally seen individuals begin to squirm in their chairs. Maybe this reaction is a commentary on American Puritanism in business. I'm not certain what the cause is, but what I do know is that many people are still made incredibly uneasy by seeing ambition or self-interest displayed publicly. Conventional wisdom says that you can't talk about what really matters to you, and though society has broken down many taboos over the past twenty-five years, ambition and compensation are still two major areas that many of us are uncomfortable discussing publicly. Why?

Could it be that many of those from my generation, particularly women, have been brought up to be nice, not make waves, and be supportive? Think about the role models women of my generation and those before me had as they grew up: teachers, nurses, caretakers, cooks, stewardesses, and mothers—all careers focused on serving others. As women grew up with those role models, the message that became ingrained was that helping others, even if it meant doing themselves a disservice, was the ideal. This is another reason why embracing the notion of being your own advocate, of championing your own needs, wants, and desires, can be foreign and for some of us even distasteful. A friend of mine shared a story with me that perfectly illustrates how mothers and fathers from previous generations viewed gender roles and the personality or behavioral characteristics that were appropriate for girls versus boys. This view had a direct effect on how she behaves in the office today.

As a high school student, my friend had jointly purchased, with a friend, a gift for one of her teachers. Unfortunately for her, the friend never ponied up her half of the expense. So the final semester rolled by, still no repayment. On the last day of school, my friend phoned the other girl and told her to bring the money with her to school that day. Her father, overhearing this, told her that the comment "wasn't nice." Basically, what he was saying was that it was okay for my friend to be out fifty dollars and be manipulated by the other girl, as long as she did it with poise. Too often, I find that grace and poise are overrated—unless you're using these qualities to improve your station at work or in a relationship. If being polite is a virtue, how does that affect getting what you want and advocating for yourself in today's work environment? Should you not ask for a raise because it isn't nice? Being aggressive at work can be a double-edged sword. Women who go after what they want are too often given a variety of negative labels. A little later in this chapter, I'll talk about generational and gender differences and how that impacts communication.

As for my friend, she took the desire to be polite too far; she couldn't see that at work it had transformed her into a manager who was uneasy demanding that others carry their fair share of the workload. She would often make excuses for her subordinates when they demonstrated a lack of follow-through or attention to detail. What she didn't realize was that she wasn't being polite, she was being an ineffective manager. Her weakness wasn't helping them get any better, and she certainly wasn't helping herself, as she was seen as weak and ineffective. Leadership and success are not about being the most polite; sometimes they're just about commanding a good offense.

So how can you, regardless of gender, implement a good offense as you pursue your flip? I'm not suggesting that you act like an arrogant oaf as you try to get your way; I am saying that you can think of your best interests first and make yourself the priority, without being an arrogant oaf. Let me stress that this belief, along with the tools in this chapter, are not intended to oppress anyone. You are not necessarily hurting someone else by looking out for yourself. The tools in this chapter are meant to either level the playing field so that you can compete effectively or create a strategic advantage for you when you are being manipulated. Being offensive allows you to turn the tables and flip the script when others are derailing you. And in case you are wondering why you should be first in line, to that I ask, "Why not you?" Another way to think about this is to consider that success is not limited. Here's how I like to think about it.

THE ROWBOAT

I often tell people to think about success more like a cruise ship than a rowboat. More often than not, people view accomplishment like a rowboat, on which there are only a limited number of seats. And on this rowboat, if you accomplish something or achieve your goals, somehow your success takes something away from someone else or knocks them off the boat. This happens all the time in our home and work lives. Think about it, and be honest: isn't this the attitude your colleagues have when someone else in the office gets promoted? On the surface people may say they are happy for them, but are they really? My experience has shown that underneath the facade, more often than not, people become bothered, annoyed, and resentful. Someone else's success becomes a threat to them.

What about closer to home? Having spent many years with my three children on the playing field and in the classroom, I often wonder why, when someone's child is good at sports or in school, others have something bad to say about that child. I can't tell you the number of times I've heard a negative comment rather than a compliment directed toward a winning person or child. The reason for all of this is that people think that if a neighbor's child is good at something, it takes something away from their own child. It's as if they believe that brat has taken their kid's seat on the rowboat. This type of thinking will not help you move your flip forward.

In reality, though common, this type of thinking is absurd—and, in fact, really ugly. When people succeed at something that we desire for ourselves, we should try and find inspiration, not resentment. Don't be intimidated by those who think and act in a negative way— it's unbecoming, ugly, and not in the spirit of fair play. This kind of attitude only serves to demean and undermine you—and it fosters an unhealthy environment. Life, love, and success are not limited to a group of select individuals to the exclusion of others. You can and must believe that your success can be honest and self-motivated and does not compete with the success of anyone else. You're not hurting anyone else by bettering yourself, and you can't worry that you are taking someone else's seat if you want to be successful. That's why I like to think of success as a cruise ship, rather than as a rowboat. On a cruise ship, there are plenty of seats and room for everyone. Don't back down and yield to others when pursuing your own goals because you feel guilty that others are less enlightened, motivated, and successful than you.

 Flip Tip: Recognize that your success does not limit others, and act accordingly.

POSITIVE MANIPULATION

There is good manipulation, and then there is bad, destructive manipulation. Understanding how and when to use controlled manipulations will take a minute to get used to. Some of them go against the good upbringing that we are often proud of. Many of us have been taught from a young age that manipulation of any sort is wrong. This, in my opinion, is a limited view. Psychological manipulation is a type of social behavior that transfers influence from one person to another in an effort to change that party's perception of one's behavior. Manipulation is typically interpreted as negative because people see it as advancing the interests of the manipulator at someone else's expense. We are taught that it is exploitative and deceptive, but this type of activity occurs all the time. For example, doctors try to persuade patients to change their unhealthy habits. The government levies heavy taxes on alcohol and other health-adverse items—so much so that they've become known as "sin taxes." Is wearing a new suit the day of a big meeting a manipulation? One can argue that such positive-minded manipulations are not bad because they are intended for the overall good of everyone involved.

That said, this book is not about achieving overall good, but it *is* about how each individual can achieve his or her own specific goals in business and in life. To do this, as I've been saying, you sometimes have to think about yourself first and make your interests a top priority. I think this approach is, at its core, honest—and this type of honesty is rarely found. In fact, hypocrisy is more often the way of the world. We see politicians rant about promoting the public good and conserving energy, and meanwhile they're flying on private jets. Or we turn on the television and hear "experts" promoting their individual agendas rather than focusing on the facts. Or what about those paid actors endorsing products? That's right, they're paid. Do you really think all those A-list actresses consistently use boxed hair color? It's obvious that such behaviors are manipulations, though they are generally done with the proposed good of a third party in mind, as in having colored hair is better than having gray hair. Advocating for yourself is more of an honest strategy in many ways—and it's not as if your intentions are hidden. With that in mind, let's consider how you can use manipulation successfully in business. You can start with a little strategic anger.

USE STRATEGIC ANGER

The first tool we will discuss in this chapter is strategic anger. Strategic anger is not reactive. It's not the feeling you experience when someone cuts you off on the highway or your meeting is canceled ten minutes before it's scheduled to start and you just spent an hour on the L.A. freeway in traffic getting there. Strategic anger is intentional—and useful—anger. It is used to let others know that you are displeased. At its most potent, it is one of the strongest weapons in gaining the advantage in any given situation. At the minimum, it will create an even playing field by shifting the balance of power. So how do you use strategic anger?

To effectively use strategic anger in the workplace, you must first come to terms with the fact that this is just business and with business there will always be an implicit imbalance of power. To win, you need to take control and hold power. Strategic anger lets you shift the balance of power in your favor. For example, imagine you have a client with whom you do business, and one day this client calls you up and he or she generously offers you a pair of tickets to an upcoming ball game or concert. You happen to be free that night, so they sound good, right?

But when you agree to accept the tickets, the balance of power shifts away from you, and it won't move back in your favor until you take action. Once those tickets are in your hands, you now owe your client, and although he will protest that he is happy to give the tickets to you without any expectation of reciprocation, don't fool yourself: this is business, and there is no such thing as a free lunch—or free tickets, in this case. But, if you use a little strategic anger, your chances of scoring that elusive free lunch increase more than tenfold.

As I said, in order to effectively use strategic anger you must accept that this is just business and the pair of tickets from your client wasn't actually an act of generosity but instead a means of manipulation on his or her part to gain influence or an advantage over you. That's what the entire business of "client entertaining" is built upon. So when a client calls to inquire how the game or the concert was, which he certainly will, most conversations go something like this:

Example 1

Client: Hey, how'd you like the tickets I sent over?

You: Oh, thank you, they were incredible.

Client: Were the seats okay?

You: They were amazing, we had such a good time, thank you so much.

Client: No, I was happy to do it. Did Sally and the kids have a good time?

You: They did, she can't stop talking about it.

Where's the most power? It's clearly in the hands of your client. And when the next tough conversation comes around about prices or late fees—and inevitably it does—you start off on your back foot, and everybody knows you can't throw a good punch off your back foot.

Strategic anger relieves this problem; it can help you level the playing field or take the lead in the relationship. I'll warn you now, strategic anger isn't easy to express; it demands that you let go of all the good manners and proper etiquette you were taught as a child. Rather than allow yourself to be manipulated, strategic anger helps you foil another's attempted manipulation. Let's revisit the conversation with your client after you've used the tickets. If your desire is to simply level the playing field, the conversation could go something like this:

<u>Example 2</u>

Client: Hey, how'd you like the tickets I sent over?

You: Oh yeah . . . (pause)

Client: Were the seats okay?

You: Well, it was loud, but it was fine, thanks.

Client: Oh, sorry to hear that . . . that's too bad. Did Sally and the kids have a good time?

You: They did, but you know, but it got to be a little past the kids' bedtime and they just got cranky.

Client: Too bad, well maybe we can plan something better next time.

You: That would be nice, maybe. Thanks again.

Do you think major CEOs are successful in reaching their goals by being the best-mannered person at the bargaining table? No, they reach their goals and find success by flipping the script and creating advantages for themselves. So again I ask, why not you? What you did with this example was to "withhold praise"—which was the manipulation your client was not expecting. People expect you to praise them for generous acts. But ask yourself, was their original offer really generous? Or was it meant to manipulate you into feeling like you owed them something? Strategic anger, at its best, can be used to put the advantage clearly in your corner. Here's how that conversation would play out if you decided to do more than just level the playing field and use strategic anger as a way of gaining power.

<u>Example 3</u>

Client: Hey, how'd you like the tickets I sent over?

You: I hate to complain.

Client: Why? What happened? Were the seats okay?

You: Not really, the seats were in a bad spot and it was tough to see, and the music was really loud, I'm not kidding. I think I lost some of my hearing. I may go to the doctor.

Client: Oh, my God, I am so sorry. I feel terrible. Are you okay? Did Sally and the kids have a good time?

You: Her ears are still bothering her, too.

Client: Oh, I feel terrible. What can I do?

Bingo. The power has shifted directly back to you. In fact, a new study in the *Journal of Consumer Research* confirms that *gaming emotions,* as the authors call it, works. Eduardo B. Andrade and Teck-Hua Ho of the University of California at Berkeley set out to examine this phenomenon, described as the act of either concealing a current emotional state or displaying one that diverges from one's true state, in an attempt to improve a social interaction. The researchers had reason to believe that consumers game emotions to benefit somehow—mostly financially—by influencing a third party.

To confirm their hypothesis, they developed several experiments to test emotion gaming. In one experiment, participants, who were told that their payment was contingent on the outcome of two tasks, played two games involving interactive decision making. In one game, the Dictator Game, a "proposer" was endowed with a pot of money to be split with the "receiver." The proposers were directed to make unfair offers, which the receivers had to accept. The Dictator Game's purpose was to create anger. And participants would keep track of this through an "anger report."

After recording their anger levels during the Dictator Game, participants played another game, the Ultimatum Game (UG), meant to simulate a retail situation in which a proposer offers a division of money and a receiver has to accept or reject it. However, a rejected offer meant that both players earned nothing. "The UG can also capture the very last phase of a complex negotiation involving multiple stages (e.g., buying a new car) where one party gives the final take-it-or-leave-it offer before walking away from the negotiation table," the authors explained.

Half of the receivers were informed that their last anger report would be shown to proposers before the proposers made offers. The results showed that receivers inflated their levels of anger when they knew that proposers would see their anger display before deciding on an offer. And the receivers readily acknowledged their strategic displays of emotions, believing them to be persuasive signals.

The results showed that "Receivers do get a better offer from proposers as long as proposers have reason to believe that their partners' feelings are genuine. When proposers learn that receivers might be inflating anger, the impact of emotion gaming on proposers' offers goes away." What this tells us is that anger can be a powerful negotiating tool. When people in the experiment felt that the anger was real, they made offers that benefited the receiver; strategic anger works.

What can we learn from this that can help us in our quest to flip the script? In either a business or personal situation, strategic anger is a useful tool to use when trying to level or change the balance of power. It can be used like a dial: you can turn it up or tune it down depending on the amount of heat necessary to accomplish your desired goal. To use strategic anger effectively, it has to be believable or based in reality, so that the other side understands that it's genuine. This means the punishment must fit the crime. Using our earlier example, being given seats to a concert can't throw you into a rage, or you will lose all credibility and maybe some relationships along the way. It's called strategic anger because it has to be used strategically. A little can go a long way. Try it.

SPEAK THE OTHER PERSON'S LANGUAGE

If strategic anger is meant to help you gain control in business interactions, the next tool is meant to help you secure supporters. If you want to achieve a goal and you are going to need another person's support to do it, you have to figure out how to speak that person's language. There are a few ways you can shape your style, tone, and message so that it will be received in the best possible way and so that ultimately you can use your relationships to achieve your goals. Keep in mind that some people, depending on their personality or how they communicate, may not respond to strategic anger—and it could backfire, which is why you need more than one technique in your arsenal. With that in mind, if you want to influence someone or a situation in your favor, you have to know your audience. By that I mean you need to have an understanding of the personality type of the people you're trying to influence. With that information, you can cater your message or approach so that it will be acceptable to them.

Identifying personality types has been a field of study since Carl Jung did his pioneering work in the area in the late 1800s and early 1900s. Jung is known for creating the field of analytical psychology, which included the notion of "psychological types." "Personality type" of an individual refers specifically to how he or she interacts with the world and how he or she processes information internally. For example, your personality type can be determined based on questions such as "Are you an extravert or an introvert?" "Do you use intuition when taking in information and making decisions, or are you data-driven?" The desire to know more about how personality affects our business relationships continued to grow, but in the beginning most of the data was not clearly organized. Thankfully, along came Paul P. Mok, who in the 1970s developed a system for determining types of communicators called Communicating Styles Technology (CST). Mok created the Communicating Styles survey, which has been given to millions of individuals in more than five thousand companies around the world. The results of the survey helped Mok validate his findings and develop ways in which organizations can improve their culture, communication, teamwork, and results. We'll talk more about culture in the next chapter. Based on CST, Mok narrowed down the list of personalities and communication styles to just four: Feelers, Sensors, Thinkers, and Intuitors.

The better you can figure out the type of person you are communicating with, the better your chance of gaining the advantage.

Mok refined his methods working in very complex organizations where adversarial thinking was the norm, such as Bank of America, AT&T, and Sun Microsystems. Executive coaches, HR professionals, leadership experts, and the like have cited Mok's work and shaped their own approaches around these four personality types. To create a support system of colleagues—allies, if you will—you need to spend some time figuring out who you're dealing with. And what type you yourself are.

Feelers

As the word implies, Feelers are empathetic. As communicators, Feelers express emotion verbally. They want to make you feel comfortable and secure and will go out of their way to help you. So when dealing with a Feeler, stress the importance of that person's assistance: "Listen, Ned, I really need the team on board with this project. I know that it will cause us to work over the weekend and put in a couple of late nights, but it can be really good for the group if we all pull together. What do you think would be the best way of getting the team's buy-in?"

Sensors

Then there are Sensors, who are focused on to-do lists and deadlines. Sensors may not have the gift of gab, particularly if they perceive your conversation as distracting them from getting something done. Communications coaches advise that when speaking with a Sensor you get to the point quickly and underscore how you can help reduce that person's workload or expedite a project for him or her. Coaches suggest that you prepare in advance of your conversation and have that script in your head: "Dan, I know that adding this new project to our team's workload is a burden. I think this would be a great opportunity to get some of the young associates involved at a higher level. How about we create assignments for each of them, and that will free you up to focus on strategy."

Thinkers

Thinkers are all about the numbers. They are logical, practical, and realistic and like solving problems. Inaccuracies are a cause for concern, and sometimes they don't get the bigger vision. So in talking to them, you must emphasize the bottom line, with specific figures: "Cindi, this project will help our team bring in an extra $250,000 in revenue this month. That amount could move the needle and put us in a good position for beating our end-of-the-year targets. Can you put a workflow model into place that tracks everyone's assignments and deliverables over the next week so we meet our deadline?"

Intuitors

Intuitors are the polar opposite of Thinkers; they are focused on the big picture and keep long-term goals in mind. They are not extremely process-oriented, so don't rely on Intuitors to come up with immediate solutions to a problem or manage deadlines—keep them focused on generating ideas, then you and your team of Thinkers and Sensors can figure out if the new venture being proposed is doable. Try an approach like this: "Stefano, we have this project under control. Now, let's think about what will drive revenue in the next fiscal year. We've made good inroads with some of our new digital products. What new markets can we get into where these products will take off?"

• • •

Knowing how to leverage someone else's personality and style for your benefit is a critical factor in building the alliances you need to achieve your flip. Let's take this a step further and think about what motivates certain communication styles. I've often found that people's generation—the decade that spanned their formative years—has a strong affect on their perceptions and attitudes. Communication styles are a combination of nature and nurture.

WHEN YOU WERE BORN MATTERS

I think it's fair to say that today's workforce is dominated by baby boomers and millennials, two generations with sharp contrasts. Baby boomers (people born between 1945 and 1960, give or take a year or two) have been characterized as confident and self-reliant, possessing the belief that they can make meaningful change. They are goal-oriented and extremely workcentric; they strive to win. They are well acquainted with the office structure and are resourceful in navigating it to achieve their goals—they do have a keen understanding of the importance of face time. That is probably the starkest difference between millennials and boomers.

Millennials (born roughly between 1980 and 2000) are incredibly technology-savvy and were likely introduced to digital devices from day one. They prefer to tweet, email, and use social networks to establish and maintain relationships. This presents a challenge to effective communicating between the generations; if you are a millennial, you risk the chance of miscommunication if you rely solely on your cell phone or computer to speak with friends, family, or colleagues, and if you're a boomer, you might consider this type of back-and-forth to be frustrating and counterproductive. If you are a baby boomer, it's up to you to mentor younger colleagues so that they can build critical interpersonal skills. But you can use their love of technology as a reward. Keep in mind that millennials are extremely entrepreneurial and don't have the acceptance of hierarchy that you might have. Some might interpret this as a sense of false entitlement. It's important to move past that perspective and help them develop the drive and social skills that will help your efforts. For example, if you can give them assignments that build on their technological skills, all the better. And if you are a millennial, it will help you to understand that baby boomers are all around you at work. They may be your boss, or they may even be your cube mate colleague who is having a second career. Finding common ground can help you with your flip. Boomers view the world differently from you. They are the generation who coined the phrase "workaholics," and many of them think work comes before everything else, including family and friends. Understand that they are extremely committed and value loyalty, but they are also adaptable to change, and if you can show them how to build a smarter way to work together, most boomers are prochange.

 Flip Tip: Know your audience; to build alliances, speak their language.

My last word of advice on this, whether you are a boomer or a millennial, is to communicate as a leader would: build alliances and increase your presence and influence. These skills, which we'll talk about in the next section, will work in your personal life as well. Think about your extended family: it includes all ages, lots of personalities, and probably a healthy dose of dysfunction. What actions will help you keep the peace and move your goals and objectives forward? If one of your goals is getting along better with your family, I remember a specific example when I took some of my own advice to heart and it really worked well. Dealing with a family's various personalities and lifestyles when sharing stories from the past is fun, but sometimes it's difficult dealing with each other in the present. We all can be guilty of casting judgment, especially when it comes to interactions between generations. I was raised in a large, church-on-Sunday type of Catholic family. My father was one of thirteen children. Whenever the extended family got together, invariably within ten minutes fights between my aunts, uncles, brothers and sisters, and me would arise. One such argument centered on the validity of "couples living together versus marrying" or "couples having children versus not having children"—each side defending its generational views. As we got older, the family gatherings seemed like all stress and no fun until I started practicing active listening. We'll also talk later about how active listening can play a role in better negotiations.

USE ACTIVE LISTENING

I could have argued my point all day, but I wouldn't have been able to change their generational opinion, and, conversely, they were not changing mine. We were just not communicating. I needed to understand where they were coming from as a generation. I needed to hear what was motivating their opinions. So one day, rather than falling back into the same routines, I decided to just shut up and listen. I practiced "active listening" rather than what I call "passive listening." What is active listening? It is when you are in the moment and have cleared your mind of other thoughts and counterarguments, a state of mind in which you can actually take in what is being said to you. Passive listening is the opposite: it occurs when you are not speaking but already have an idea in your head and are just waiting for the other person to stop talking so you can speak again. You are not actually listening to the person; there is a big difference. Active listening works this way: you allow the person, in my case my older aunt, who believed that couples should not live together before marriage, to make a statement. You do not respond immediately; in fact, you must wait for a minimum of three seconds to consider what was just said. The next step requires that rather than making a counterargument to that statement, you ask a question. So the difference in the dialogue may look a bit like this:

Example 1: Passive Listening

Aunt: Kids today shouldn't live together before getting married.

Me: You don't understand, things are different today from when you grew up.

Aunt: Yeah, we had values—we weren't running around hopping into bed.

Me: Maybe that's why 50 percent of marriages end in divorce.

Aunt: We didn't get divorced in our day either, you got married and that was it.

Me: Forget it.

Sound familiar? You can see from this example that neither side is listening to the other. The conversation is going nowhere. But whether in the family or at work, understanding another person's generational perspective is a valuable asset in building alliances. This type of scenario occurs daily in most office environments. Though the subject matter may be less personal, the results are the same. When neither side is listening, you are not moving your goals forward. Remember, you can't control other people, and you may need their support in the future, so you have to find a way to build consensus; with that in mind, let's try the same conversation with active listening:

Example 2: Active Listening

Aunt: Kids today shouldn't live together before getting married.

[*Pause:* three seconds]

Me (question): Why do you think that?

Aunt: You have no commitment; you see all the bad before you even get married.

[*Pause:* three seconds]

Me (question): So do you think that if a person really knows you first, they won't marry you?

Aunt: Maybe not; marriage is hard work.

[*Pause:* three seconds]

Me: I agree, and I'm looking for all the help I can get, so if you've got some advice I'm all ears.

You can see from active listening that each side did not have to lose his or her point of view on the subject. I could still keep my beliefs, but listening allowed me to build consensus and have my aunt feel that she was truly being heard. There is no end to the value of learning to be an effective communicator. You can use these skills to flip your script as a leader in your family room or in the boardroom.

 Flip Tip: Try active listening when attempting to build consensus.

I COMMUNICATE, THEREFORE I LEAD

Effective, purposeful communication (essentially, putting your money where your mouth is) plays a strong role in your ability to act like a leader. Regardless of your position within a company, demonstrating the skills of someone who can rally the troops, putting words into action, and maintaining a smoothly running machine can only help you make your flip. That is something you can do right now; anyone who strives to achieve good communication is already acting in a leadership role.

Along with effective communication, another essential element of building a supportive work environment is trust. If you can create trust with someone and communicate persuasively, that person will go the extra mile for you—and become a collaborator in helping you achieve your flip rather than an adversary. We live in a different professional reality than our parents, who would work for the same company for their entire career. In our world, every job counts and the dynamics in the work environment brought on by global competition and advances in technology have raised the stakes for each of us. Persuasion and trust will serve you well in this new reality. The average person today will work for three companies in the course of his or her career. Each time you begin in a new position, you have an opportunity to build new alliances, garner support, and collaborate effectively. The difference is not just the number of people you have to get along with, it's where they are located. Technology and globalization have altered the playing field. You may not have the luxury of building morale by going out for a drink after work or popping down the hall to chat about the weekend. As is common in work today, the team you are working alongside may not be physically next to you. You may be finding yourself Skyping with colleagues in China or India, making building a supportive work environment all the more vital.

I've talked about getting to know the attributes of those you are speaking to, the traits to keep in mind as you frame your communications, the generational differences you may come up against, and the way you can elevate your effort by assuming the traits of a leader. These are all good skills to have, but what should you do when someone actively works against you? How can you break through unwelcome behavior, conflict, and confrontation so that you come out on top?

BAD APPLES

As I mentioned earlier, there are people out there who resent anyone else's accomplishments, and I would say that a certain percentage of them will not willingly support you and in fact might try to thwart your every move. Those folks are toxic, and although you are right not to want to make them your best friends, you need to handle them strategically. Strategic anger will likely backfire, as they're likely to use all of their power or influence to undermine you. Empathy will make you seem weak to them, giving them an opening to contradict you in meetings, bad-mouth you to the boss, steal your clients, or lay claim to your successes. For many of us, this is the reality we face in our daily lives. Whether at home, at work, or within a relationship, you do sometimes have to deal with combative people. A lot of books published on this topic stress the need to establish trust—come to a meeting of the minds, if you will—and forge some kind of collaborative effort. Remember, this is a chess game; gaining the trust of your opponent is great if it both serves your purpose and helps *you*.

With that in mind, I'm going to suggest an approach called the CRIB method, created by the founders of Vital Smarts, Kerry Patterson and Joseph Grenny. What follows is my take on CRIB. It is designed to help you establish trust and develop alliances. The method is broken down into four steps:

- **C**ommit to seeking a mutual purpose. The only thing that an adversary wants more than to see you fail is to improve his or her own station. Build on that desire and devise a way for both of you to succeed. That way, your toxic comrade will not see your success as collateral damage. In this early stage of the process, you're not coming up with a mutual purpose; you're just agreeing to find one.

- **R**ecognize the purpose behind the strategy. If you're getting pushback, try to determine why. Try to talk it through with the other person. If, for example, he or she asks, "Why wouldn't you want to share your monthly report with me?" be honest: "Well, in the past I've seen clients of mine pop up on your report." Or "I've noticed that after I announce a project you seem to pursue similar ventures."

- **I**nvent a mutual purpose. If you can't easily see what the mutual purpose is, invent one. Maybe your spouse wants a date night in the city once a month, but you commute there every day during the week and making the trip even once a month on a weekend is completely unappealing. But for your spouse, being isolated from that part of your world is disconcerting. What's the joint purpose of date night? What's your long-term goal? Identify that and then figure out how you can achieve that goal within both of your parameters.

- **B**rainstorm new strategies. With a mutual purpose now created, how are you going to execute? This is the hard part. If you thought that coming up with a mutual purpose was difficult, working through a solution for achieving it will be painful—even more if you are dealing with contentious parties. When that happens, move out of angry conversations and remind the other person of your mutual purpose: "We both want to help the group succeed. The better we make our boss look, the better senior management will think of us."

You now have a sense of how to develop alliances and deal with difficult people, but what if you find yourself in an environment that is foreign to you? How do you even begin to understand how people think, communicate, and perceive? In the next chapter, we'll learn about the ROPE method, which is designed to help you adapt to every type of cultural dynamic.

Chapter 7

The **ROPE** Method

Whosoever desires constant success must
change his conduct with the times.
—NICCOLÒ MACHIAVELLI

IN THIS CHAPTER I will discuss the various types of cultures and personalities you may encounter in your work and personal lives and help you learn how to figure out which type of culture you're in. You'll also learn how to use that knowledge to help move your flip forward. Acclimating to your environment or culture is an important step in making your flip—but fitting in is not without its challenges.

Most of us are told at a young age that we should always be ourselves, and at some level, of course, this is wise advice and a good way to behave. But when does being too attached to your own way of doing things threaten to derail your business or personal needs and goals? I like to think of the opportunities we are given at work as ropes. If managed successfully, they can be used to pull yourself up the ladder or to create ties that bind you closely, and in a healthy way, to others. But maneuvering through rough corporate, or even family, waters at times can be treacherous; personalities, culture, and ego all play dynamic parts. Flipping your script and achieving your goals demand that you understand and navigate through even the toughest of cultural seas successfully—so be careful, because the same rope that you use to climb high, if not managed correctly, can become a rope that ties you up politically and restricts your flip.

Remember, no person is an island; flipping isn't only about you, it involves everyone else around you. You are part of a culture, whether you like it or not. In this chapter I'll show you the tools that will help you best adapt to and use the culture you're in to your benefit.

I'll present the ROPE method, designed to help you climb higher in your career and avoid dangerous entanglements. The ROPE method is an approach to navigating and staying focused on completing your flip. It will help you identify and avoid cultural clashes and gain confidence through a series of behaviors, including role modeling, openness to change, projecting confidence, and exuding humility. In addition, we will tackle how each step in the ROPE method can play an integral part in getting you through all of the challenges you may face while flipping. Before we get into the specifics of the ROPE approach, we need to understand what "culture" is and why it plays such an important role in flipping.

PARLEZ-VOUS FRANÇAIS?

If you're reading this chapter and thinking "I don't need this, I've got my situation figured out," all I ask you to do is to go back and look at why you haven't yet achieved your flips. Consider the old poem about the six blind men and the elephant. If you don't recall it, there are six blind men, and they are all touching an elephant. Each has a different idea about what the elephant is like, based on the part of the animal he is touching. Each is convinced that he is right. And essentially they are all right; none is wrong, but each has his own experience of the truth. But they don't come to that realization, each thinking the others in the group are mistaken. The inability to see situations from others' perspectives is one of the major pitfalls I see many of my colleagues and peers fall into as they pursue their goals. They mistakenly believe that everyone speaks the same language—figuratively, that is. Well, let me tell you, they don't. I often advise colleagues to imagine that they speak French and the people they are trying to impress, motivate, convince, or influence speak English. Think about it: you can talk, yell at them, seduce them, or even tell them a joke, but if they don't understand what you are saying—literally or conceptually—it's point-less. When flipping, you need to remember that every person brings his or her own cultural bias, history, insights, and values into any discussion. Everyone has good experiences that you can learn from, along with baggage that you will want to sidestep. If you are to get the support you need to win, you can't become frustrated if others don't understand what you're saying. You have to embrace their culture. I often see an example of this when an employee receives a promotion to first-time manager. Usually the individual is promoted to manage-ment because he or she is smart, organized, and self-motivated. Such individuals stand out among their peers. But I've seen even the bright-est employees struggle with the transition from being personally mo-tivated to motivating others. Appreciating that we are all wired and motivated differently and that to get the best out of yourself and mo-tivate others you need to see things from their perspective, is essential to success.

The same set of strategies can apply to both business and life. Think about it: what new activity have you participated in recently? Whether it was playing a new sport, traveling to a foreign city, or even learning a new game of cards, the first thing you needed to do was learn the rules of the game. As you embarked on the endeavor, you probably considered the following questions: What equipment do I need to play? What are the rules? How does one score? Most of us understand that to win we must follow the rules. So when you think about building your career or having a better personal relationship, you should ask yourself: how can I score if I don't know which way to run or who gets the ball?

In sports and most other formal games, the rules are usually easy to follow because they are written down and don't change from player to player. But rules at work or in personal relationships are much harder to wrap your head around. They aren't typically writ-ten down and are not always clear or consistent. No one says, "I don't speak French, and I can't understand what you are saying." They usually just roll their eyes and walk away—or it can be more subtle than that. Work culture and interpersonal relationships more often rely on unwritten customs and varying social behaviors, both of which are easily open to interpretation. To achieve your flip, you need to become adept at identifying the rules of whatever culture you find yourself in and being flexible so that you can move from your own style to one that matches your new environment.

GAINING THE HOME-FIELD ADVANTAGE

In the last chapter we discussed key offensive tactics, such as strategic anger, and the role they play in the process of flipping the script. They can and will help you score. But as any athlete knows, you can practice all week long and give it your best, but who wouldn't give up an extra day of practice in exchange for having the home-field advantage?

What is the home-field advantage in business and in life? I would argue that it is being aware of and understanding the culture that surrounds you. Having the home-field advantage means that you are able to manage the players within the environment and community and be seen as an active, vital member. There are idiosyncratic cultures in every situation. Culture is not limited to corporations. There are cultures in neighborhoods and on playgrounds. There is a culture at the golf club. And most certainly there is a culture within any family or office.

With regard to families, each has its own set of rules and customs that makes perfect sense to its members but less-than-perfect sense to outsiders. Years ago, when a friend's sister was newly married, she would spend countless hours on the phone with him discussing her new in-laws and why their family customs and attitudes presented problems for her. Sound familiar? I don't recall the specifics of what they did or said, but the specifics are irrelevant because the things his sister complained about are universal. One particular holiday she was frustrated, perplexed, and upset by their approach to a holiday dinner, because what and when they ate were different from what her family had always done. She asked my friend, "Who on earth eats at 3 P.M.?" His answer was simple: "They do, and now they are your in-laws, so get used to it." If you try to fight culture, it will only leave you feeling more frustrated. In that case, my friend's sister needed to learn to speak her new in-laws' language and appreciate them and their family customs to achieve the successful, loving relationship she wanted for the sake of her husband and their children. The next holiday, rather than fighting their culture, she thought of ways to incorporate her traditions into theirs, and that has greatly improved her relationship with her in-laws.

When you start to think this way, your path becomes much easier. All you need to do is figure out the culture you find yourself in. The best way to figure it out is to look for what it values. Do you work in an organization that values entrepreneurialism and bottom-line accountability? Or is it a culture that places higher value on teamwork and collective results? Does the culture esteem bold risk taking and big personalities, or does it pride itself on being more thoughtful, quiet, and risk adverse? It may seem obvious, but I can't tell you the number of times people have called me to tell me they were leaving their current jobs for promotion and increased responsibility at another firm. Some were good cultural fits, but many more weren't. I would say, "Are you sure you can get along there? They are so type A, and you are so laid back." A year later, when they were looking for a new job, it was simply that the personality of the individual and the personality of the culture wouldn't mesh unless the person changed, because the culture of the company wasn't going to. Once you know what the culture values, you are a step closer to understanding how to manage and use it to your advantage.

"SUMMER" CAN BE A VERB

Figuring out what a culture values isn't always easy. As a young executive at Condé Nast, I lacked any real taste or sense of style. I'm not even sure I knew what "style" was. I grew up thinking that jelly jars were the good crystal and that if people had a master bathroom in the house they had made it. When I was growing up, style seemed like a luxury—and it was one we couldn't afford. But you never know where life can take you, and somehow here I was, improbably working for a company where impeccable taste and breeding were company calling cards. Talk about a cultural challenge!

I think at times we all struggle to fit in, both at work and in our personal lives. The culture of any organization may or may not be evident the minute you walk through the door; this was no doubt the case when I was younger and interviewing for my first position at the company. I had grown up with a love of magazines and a healthy awe of Condé Nast and its owner, Si Newhouse. After my interview I even wrote a follow-up letter saying that even if I didn't get the job I would die happy because I had interviewed there. A bit dramatic, certainly, but it was how I felt. But one thing that has always stuck with me from that interview was my first experience with culture shock, which occurred when I was asked where I "summered."

At first I struggled to understand what was being asked of me. I thought "summer" was a season and a noun. When did it become a verb? I was quick enough at the time to know that telling them that I "summered" at my parents' home on Long Island where I spent summers mowing lawns for twenty bucks a pop was probably not the right answer. So I said, "Long Island." "Oh yes, we're out there, too" was the reply. "Are you in East or South?" I wasn't sure, but I guessed she was referring to the Hamptons. At that point in my life, I had never been to the Hamptons, even though we lived only twenty-three miles away. "No, my parents have a place on the north shore." I was proud I hadn't lied—technically. The truth was, my parents' place was their permanent place of residence and we were miles from any "shore," but the answer seemed to suffice and the interviewer moved on. I wanted the job, and I wanted to fit in. And due to my interest in fitting in, as well as many other reasons, I got the job. Now I faced the prospect of a future filled with similar situations in which I'd have to adapt to an alien culture. It became apparent that to win, the faster I learned to be a "quick study"—that is, someone who can read culture and politics, who's in charge, who recognizes stakeholders and who has power, and who can assimilate within them—the faster I would achieve my goals.

In *Working with Emotional Intelligence,* Dan Goleman stresses the importance of not only understanding a company's culture but also its political underpinnings if you are going to thrive in it. He says that you have to work to understand the culture, alliances, and rivalries in a workplace so that you can know what issues are important to the key decision makers, because the decision makers drive the culture. So how do you read an organization—that is, how do you identify its political struggles and properly align yourself with the forces that will help you succeed?

Basically, that was the question I was faced with and the one you'll be faced with at some point in your career: How do you fit into a culture? And how do you avoid losing yourself in the process?

 Flip Tip: To identify a culture, find out what traits it values.

CULTURE CLUB?

Culture affects every part of the organization, dictating what is expected and acceptable behavior. Does work start at 7 A.M., as in the financial markets, or do people roll in with a cup of coffee at ten, as in the creative fields? Is face time important, or is it just bottom-line results that matter? Like understanding personality types, which I covered in chapter 6, identifying a culture is key to getting what you want. Let's take a moment to look at the different types of cultures.

Culture is almost always determined/dictated from the top. Think about it in your own home. You are the CEO of your own life. You decide if the kids go to bed early or you are a family that sleeps late on Sundays. You decide if you make your bed in the morning or leave it unmade all week. Are you laid back and don't care if people show up unannounced at your home, or are you a planner, scheduling everything? In your life you have created a culture that makes perfect sense to you. In the business world, the people at the top establish a cultural footprint that makes sense to them. If you are anywhere other than the top, it's not your job to change the culture, and it probably wouldn't work if you tried.

Cultures can be flexible, but they are strong. Being an agent of change while staying within the system is prized; being perceived as an outlier or instigator could hinder your success. But how can you do the right thing?

You can achieve change by having a keen awareness of the internal politics within the culture and if possible using them to your advantage. Be aware: cultures can defend themselves, and focusing solely on your own interests will ultimately create blind spots that will keep you from reaching your goals. It may also hurt your relationships with your colleagues—the very same people you need as your support system. "Political animals," people who play the culture for their exclusive benefit, are often viewed with disdain and distrust—and that will be a long-term liability. Maintaining a broader perspective is essential. There are three ways I recommend for winning at the game of office politics and using culture to advance your flip.

1. **Never complain.** There is a time and place for everything, but work is not the place to complain. It doesn't make anything better and will not help you achieve your goals. I recommend saving any grievances for home or close friends. To win at politics, you must demonstrate positive, professional conduct; this positions you as an agent of positive change and alleviates the risk of alienating others.

2. **Keep your core support.** As any good politician knows, to get elected you must think about who your key constituents are. Who are your base supporters? Maintaining a base of loyal supporters increases your microphone volume. The larger the group, the louder and more credible you become. Finding ways to build supporters can take as little as five minutes a day. I do it every day, first thing in the morning and/or in the evening before I leave: I take five minutes to shoot off an email, walk down the hall to chat, stop at someone's desk to ask

about his or her kid's graduation, weekend plans, new exercise regimen, whatever; I don't talk, I just listen and I am sincerely interested. This broader perspective reminds me daily that the people I work with are just that: people. And when I've needed to call on them for support over the years, they have been there.

3. **Keep your eye on the end goal.** In any office there are often several competing agendas, so you need to stay clear of anybody or anything that does not move your flip forward. Keep your focus, with your end goal always in sight. Try not to take sides or get caught up in others' agendas; you have no idea whose support you may need in the future.

 Flip Tip: To win at politics, don't complain, and take five minutes a day to build alliances and stay focused on your end goals.

DOES EVERY CULTURE FIT?

Like a good pair of jeans, to feel good the corporate culture has to fit you right. Every culture has a social order that reflects the personality, values, ethics, beliefs, and traits of the company's founders, its management, and ultimately its employees. Is your business a start-up with a newly emerging culture, or is it a well-established company where the culture is so strong that even newly hired senior management may not be able to change it? Whatever the corporate culture, it's up to each of us to decide if we can feel comfortable and compatible with it—or, at the very least, that we can adapt to it. If we can, we tend to stay, and if we can't, we usually leave. When thinking about allies, remind yourself that the people working alongside you generally accept the company's culture and values, and that's why they've stayed. So I'll assume that if you are working within a particular culture, either business or personal, you are doing so because you want to, and you have accepted its foundational values. If you haven't and this flip is about finding a place that better reflects your values, keep reading.

Working within your company's culture is critically important because it underlies the way business is done both inside and outside the organization. It sets expectations before anyone walks in the door. When people come and talk to me about their organizations and why they may not be succeeding, one of the first questions I ask is "What is your corporate culture?" What I mean by that is "What is it like to work there?" Intuiting a company's culture often makes the difference between success and failure. Ignoring it or assuming a contradictory position will almost surely lead to failure. I don't believe that there is a right or wrong corporate culture, but I do think that there is a right or wrong fit for each person. In order to fit into the environment and set yourself up for success, be sure that the company's values, beliefs, and ethics are compatible with yours. If you can't do that, either choose a company that shares your ideals or find a way to live with the culture as it stands. Either way, I've developed the ROPE method to help you manage through and win.

THE **ROPE** METHOD

I've taken my years of experience, my successes and failures, and tried to distill what I've learned into a four-step approach to managing culture and politics. As I mentioned in the opener to this chapter, I call this approach the ROPE method because when we are flipping to climb higher up the corporate ladder, we need to use all the tools at our disposal, and, like an actual rope, the ROPE method is a useful, sturdy ally.

1. **R**ole Model

We could all use a good role model. Whether they know it or not, role models can play a vital part in helping us move ahead in business and in our personal lives. Role models can be any person whom you can look to for insight, mentoring, or inspiration. I like to think of role models as life's CliffsNotes; they are people who have already done the hard work, and you can use their understanding to gain insight and help you achieve your objectives much more quickly than if you were on your own. Effective role models help provide a blueprint for navigating the maze of life.

Unfortunately, in the professional world finding a role model has become increasingly difficult. I believe that this is due to two main reasons. First, as I mentioned earlier, more and more professionals in a highly mobile workforce do not view it as their responsibility to manage others' career growth and development. And second, as job responsibilities morph, many people find themselves in organizational roles that are newly created, meaning that they have no peers with previous relevant experience.

In life, finding a mentor or role model can prove even more difficult. For many of us, life is completely different from what we experienced growing up. The world has changed so much that the examples your parents or family may have set may no longer be relevant. So what can you do?

YOU DON'T NEED ADVICE; YOU NEED *GOOD ADVICE*

A good role model will help you separate "advice," which is plentiful but often useless and sometimes harmful, from "good advice," which is the healthy alternative. Good advice comes from individuals who have achieved success in a particular area and can share their life experience and personal insights. Would you go to a baker to ask about your muffler? Of course not. So apply this line of thinking to life and business.

To illustrate this point, I'll tell a story about my good friend Liz and something that happened to her years ago but that has always stayed with me. When she graduated from college, she secured an entry-level position as a recruiter at a major investment firm. She was thrilled and could see herself quickly rising and getting a corner office. But ambition can be blinding. As is the case with many young recent college grads, she was dynamic but inexperienced. Prone to high drama and without a solid role model, she was headed for the same misstep many young professionals make. Liz could be charming, but she still hadn't fully grasped office dynamics. One day when I was sitting in her family's kitchen, she came home and told her mother and father about some conflict she was having with a peer. The woman was becoming an office rival, and it was clear that the two of them disagreed on most things. The rival had worked in the office for more than five years.

Liz felt that she had developed a great relationship with her boss, who oversaw both her and her rival. She believed that she and her boss were friends. She came home one day to seek advice from her parents. Now, it's important to note that both of her parents were academics and had never worked in an office environment. They advised her to go into her boss's office and demand that the other employee be "spoken to" about her obvious lack of talent. What they didn't take into consideration was the rival's own great relationship with her boss, which had been built over the five years he had worked for the company or, perhaps, that demanding a colleague be reprimanded and causing her boss more work can reflect poorly on you—especially if you are doing it for dubious, competitive reasons. She took her parents' advice, and the strategy backfired, ultimately costing Liz her job.

Though it's nearly certain that your parents love you, it does not mean that they are the best role models to follow in managing your career. One of the main reasons parents fail as role models is that they're not objective, and giving good advice requires objectivity. Objectivity isn't always easy to find but at work can most often be found in someone more senior to you rather than a peer. The reason is that senior executives have a broader perspective to give advice from; they must balance your needs and interests with the needs of the organization. This gives them a more objective perspective, like that of a good coach, who needs to think about both the good of the individual players and the collective good of the team. They may be more critical, but that criticism can often be your best friend and a powerful tool to growth. But not all senior executives are the same, so identify people who share some values with you—like attracts like—and then use their behavior and ideas as a guide for what you should be doing.

In doing this it's important to note the differences between role models and mentors.

In my experience, *role models* are people I know and observe, people who have had an influence on me, but with whom, for whatever reason—schedules, hierarchy, access—I've not developed a close personal relationship. They are people I see succeeding in life and doing it in a way that I esteem and value. I might have met the person once in a meeting, or it might be a colleague I see regularly. The trait that makes them worthy role models could be something as complicated as observing how they find balance between their home and work lives or as simple as the fact that they never seem flustered, rushed, or stressed and always have a smile on their faces. They offer ideas and ideals for behavior in their actions and reaffirm to me that I can be successful by making the same types of choices. I have several of these types of role models, some of whom are unaware of their impact on me as an executive. One example who comes to mind is a senior executive I often used to watch interacting in the cafeteria years ago, when I first started at Condé Nast. He was a powerful player at the company and was impeccably dressed each day. He always seemed so natural, so comfortable in his own skin and down to earth; I admired that. I would watch as he waited in the food line with his tray, taking time to talk to even the lowest-level employees of the company, all the time laughing and asking them questions. Although I never met him personally, he became a role model. I wanted to be just like him. From what I witnessed, his easy, straightforward approach to dealing with people remained the same whether he was interacting with the CEO or the janitor. His influence as a role model, an ideal I wanted to follow, has played a major role in shaping my management style today. Look around you: who are your role models?

Mentors, on the other hand, can play a role that is deeper than just presenting behavior ideals. They are role models on steroids. They are the individuals whom I talk to about the things that are on my mind, whom I approach with questions. It is an expanded relationship that includes the personal. Mentors are people with whom you can talk honestly about complicated issues you struggle with. Their value is not just in their observed behavior; it comes from a deeper respect that stems from their advice, their patience, and the fact that they've known me over time and can provide a cumulative perspective. They are individuals with whom I associate regularly, and they often become close friends over time. Thankfully, I have several of those, too. Who are the role models and mentors in your life? Take a minute to write down ten things you value about them. And if you don't have one yet, don't worry; I'll show you how you can build your role model network.

How can you go about finding good role models and mentors? What follows are the four steps I've used with great success to identify and connect with such valuable individuals.

Step 1: Start with respect. Start off with the people you respect, not just the people you like and want to grab a drink with but those whom you honestly respect. Think of who is the person you would most be afraid to displease. That is someone you respect. Friends and family really don't work here: respect comes from a different place and is not necessarily based on shared interests or history.

Step 2: Be a sponge. The more you absorb, watch, and learn, the closer you'll get to the core principles of the behaviors of the people you respect, and that's really what you're seeking. You want a role model who has a proven track record. The best way to find one is to watch for behaviors you like and respect and figure out why they occur. For instance, "Why does everyone else stop talking when they speak?" When you start to really *understand* how they're doing certain things, you can begin to do them as well.

Step 3: Be choosy. The role model's expertise must match the area in which you are seeking guidance. This sounds simple, but just because someone is good in one area does not make him or her good in another. Make certain your role models or mentors match up with your needs.

Step 4: Be your own judge. Don't follow people blindly. Apply what you already know and your preexisting sense of what works and doesn't work to the advice you get. That's not to say you shouldn't try out new ideas, and we'll talk more about that in a minute; just don't take everything you are told at face value. You need to put your own spin on things. This is about *your life and career,* no one else's, so make your own judgments.

 Flip Tip: Find mentors and role models whose life and work experience matches your needs.

2. Open Yourself to Change

I can't stress enough how important it is to remain open to change when you're flipping in a culture. You can always tell when someone hasn't traveled much. Those who haven't witnessed other cultures often think anything different from what they know is "weird." This attitude is called "fear of the unknown," and when you rise above it, it speaks directly to your level of personal sophistication. The problem with fear of the unknown is that it can cause you to get stuck in your own way of doing things and therefore limit your ability to immerse yourself in new cultures. Recent research has proved that people who are more open cope better with change and succeed at higher levels.

In a study conducted in 2000, published in the *Journal of Applied Psychology,* researchers Connie R. Wanberg and Joseph T. Banas used a longitudinal study to examine predictors of employee openness (i.e., change acceptance and positive view of changes). They found that personal resilience (a composite of self-esteem, optimism, and perceived control) was related to higher levels of change acceptance. As they put it, "Three context-specific variables (information received about the changes, self-efficacy for coping with the changes, and participation in the change decision process) were predictive of higher levels of employee openness to the changes and as a result employee success. Lower levels of change acceptance were associated with less job satisfaction, more work irritation, and stronger intentions to quit." What this tells us is that openness to change is important because the more open to change you are, the more adaptable you are and thus the more successful you can become.

The field of positive psychology also underscores the importance of being resilient and maintaining a healthy attitude toward change in being successful at your endeavors. Aspects of this field have found their way into popular business writing and with good reason. Let's face it: the world is becoming more complicated, with unexpected changes thrust upon us every day. You need to keep yourself mentally prepared to handle both expected and unforeseen changes—good and bad—that come your way. It's not good enough to have a Plan A and Plan B; you also need to consider Plans C, D, and E. The more prepared you are, the more resilient you'll be when change does come your way. When dealing with sudden and multiple changes, go back to what we talked about in earlier chapters, and practice the "So what?" technique; reread those chapters and allow yourself to see new options, and you will begin to be able to create new opportunities.

Being open and resilient is only part of the equation. You also have to project confidence and show that you are not only fitting in but thriving and ready to rise.

3. Project Confidence

In face-to-face interactions, self-confidence—not power—may be the ultimate skill or relationship builder because of the way it so effectively puts others at ease, often without their even knowing it. Self-confidence is the internal belief in one's self and abilities. Projecting self-confidence is critical to the process of flipping the script because when you project self-confidence, not only are you more likely to gain support from your peers, clients, and management, it also has a trickle-down effect, inspiring confidence and belief in others.

Projecting self-confidence can be an important tool in flipping and gaining personal shareholders within or outside any organization. But how can you project self-confidence if you don't feel it? To that question I say, "Sometimes you gotta fake it till you make it." Which means, try *acting* self-confident, and soon you will *be* more self-confident. Here are a few things you can do to help build your self-confidence.

LOOK GOOD

It may be one of the oldest clichés, but it's still so true: "When you look good, you feel good." So take it to heart; go beyond simply being presentable at work. Take an extra ten minutes in the morning to really think about how you will present yourself that day. Consider the following: people often feel that spending too much time thinking about how they look or what they'll wear indicates excessive vanity or self-absorption. I disagree. They argue that it's what's inside that counts. And although I agree that what's inside matters most, I think that most people won't get to see what's inside if you're not confident about what's outside. Let's face it, there's no better person to invest in than yourself. Think about it: you spend money and time on your home, your car, your children. It's time you think about your clothes, your hair, your maintenance as a career investment—in yourself. The better you feel about yourself, the more self-confidence you will project.

 Flip Tip: Dress for the job you want, not for the job you have.

BE AWARE OF YOUR BODY LANGUAGE

Did you ever watch a politician give a great speech? Each gesture is discussed and managed in advance to project paramount self-confidence and self-control. Do you know anybody who projects self-confidence while incessantly fidgeting? I doubt it. That kind of nervous behavior not only draws negative attention to you but makes others nervous watching it. Your body language can speak volumes; ultimately you want people's attention to be on what you are saying, not what you are doing. Projecting self-confidence means keeping your fidgeting to a minimum. One of the ways to accomplish this is to keep your hands down and away from your face. Try establishing an invisible line some-where around your torso and keeping your hands below it. It may feel unnatural at first, but it works. Stand with your hands resting at your sides, or, if that is too difficult, clasp your hands at your waist. Practice in front of a mirror; the more poised and calmer you appear, the more self-confidence you project.

 Flip Tip: Your body language indicates your level of self-confidence; keep your arms still and at your sides.

MAKE EYE CONTACT

One of the most powerful ways to project self-confidence is by making eye contact. It's said that the eyes are the windows to the soul; well, they are also the keys to the corner office. Over the years I have heard many a manager say, "I could never trust anyone who doesn't look me in the eyes." To gain the confidence of others, you need to look them in the eyes when you speak to them. This can be difficult for long periods of time, so try this: when you speak or listen to another person, choose a spot on his or her face to focus on, somewhere near the eyes. You want to mimic looking into the person's eyes and appear to be doing so without actually doing so. The spot can be between the eyebrows or between the eyes; it works in helping to project confidence without making someone else uncomfortable with long stares.

 Flip Tip: When making eye contact, focus not directly on the eyes, but on the other person's eyebrows.

4. Express Humility

Projecting self-confidence is important in inspiring others and garnering shareholder support, but the flip side of self-confidence is also equally valuable. Expressing humility is a strong and valuable counterbalance. Humility is your ability to show weakness, admit failure, and present the truth. When you express humility, it suggests a dimension of trustworthiness that engenders loyalty—whether the loyalty of your clients, customers, colleagues, staff, or family. Think back to your reading assignments in high school. Wasn't there always one character who was an arrogant jerk—egotistical and self-serving—and didn't that character always get his or her comeuppance by the end of the book?

The notion of hubris is an ancient concept, explored in nearly all of the writings by ancient Greek and Roman playwrights. In modern times, developing a sense of humility in business can help you in numerous ways. The two most important effects it has is that it (1) opens you up to the good ideas of others and (2) builds a more trusting relationship between you and your colleagues, friends, and family.

The benefits of humility in the workplace are discussed by the best-selling author Jim Collins; in particular in his book *Good to Great: Why Some Companies Make the Leap . . . and Others Don't,* Collins introduced the notion of the Level 5 leader. The quality that puts this leader at the top is humility, and this aspect of leadership makes good companies into great companies. Confidence without humility will not sustain success; the two need to go hand in hand. Level 5 leaders are all around us in the form of teachers, coaches, spouses, bosses, and colleagues—and it is the dash of humility that makes them special and successful.

Much has been written lately about the financial markets' collapse and how business leaders are full of hubris and lack humility. Call a leader with humility what you will—an authentic leader, servant leader, or Jesus-CEO—the ability to be respectful of others' ideas and wants can only propel you forward in building stronger relationships, being personally more productive, and guiding your team toward greater results. It always used to amaze me when I walked into companies and saw huge posters proclaiming what a kinder, gentler place this particular organization was but under the surface one would find septic managers, miserable employees, and frightened middle managers. Without humility you won't get very far. Recall my story in an earlier chapter about "know-it-all-ism," and add to that what I said about the new workforce in the last chapter; excessive blind confidence won't help you keep your peers or staff around for long, either.

The most intelligent people I've come across personally or through my media work connections have a very accurate and fair sense of their own abilities and look to others to contribute strengths or ideas they might not have. Our best political leaders surround themselves with a staff of intelligent human beings, and the same holds true for the best business leaders. Even in the world of celebrities, the artists who seem to have it all—thriving careers, strong family ties, a good head on their shoulders—seek out a network of supporters who contribute something valuable to the relationship. But having a sea of "yes-men" around you does not mean that you have a strong collaborative network. You need critical thinkers who in some circumstances might question your judgment or offer a contrary perspective. To attract intelligent individuals to your network, you need to recognize that your ideas aren't the only ones worth pursuing. Intelligent people can disagree; welcome such conversations, and approach them with an open, respectful, and humble mind. Sharing ideas, debating, and solving problems are all worthwhile pursuits that will only make you stronger in your career and personal lives.

As you move toward your flip, make these key individuals your collaborators, role models, or mentors. Humility, along with the skills noted above, will play an important role as you develop the ability to negotiate new environments or change successfully. And you have to do so without making enemies. In the next chapter I'll show you the best ways to avoid making enemies on your way up through perfecting your negotiating skills.

Chapter 8

Everything's a Negotiation

You must never try to make all the money that's in a deal.
Let the other fellow make some money too, because
if you have a reputation for always making all the
money, you won't have many deals.

—J. PAUL GETTY

AS THE SAYING GOES, "You don't get what you deserve in business; you get what you negotiate." The same could be said about flipping your script. You don't always just get what you deserve; you get what you work for. People aren't going to do what you say just because you've announced what you want. We've learned this throughout the book. In fact, our entire journey thus far has been about discovering that you have the power and insights to make things happen for yourself. The process of flipping the script—which focuses on learning to get what you want in life and feeling empowered to write your own happy ending—isn't just about being the author of the script. You need to be a great director, too. Not only do you have to write the script and manage all the actors and their egos, you also have to build the set and tell everyone where to go, what to do, and when to do it.

As a director, you must be a great negotiator who works with the crew to set the stage. It's not easy being in the director's chair, but it's incredibly empowering. In the last two chapters I gave you tools for creating an ideal environment for you to achieve your goals. But when push comes to shove and a decision needs to be made between your needs and desires and someone else's, you'll need to negotiate your way to success and remove whatever obstacles stand in your way. This is a big part of a director's job: smoothing out or resolving the stumbling blocks that threaten to keep a production on hold.

Your problem-solving arsenal wouldn't be complete without negotiation skills, especially if you wish to get rid of any obstacles that stand in your way—whether people, limitations, internal fears, or family obligations. I'll cover a variety of these obstacles and show you how to use your influence and powers of negotiation to get what you want.

Anyone who has ever been around kids at bedtime knows that learning to negotiate starts at an early age. And the kids who get to stay up to watch their favorite show don't do it by whining, yelling, or threatening. Effective negotiation relies on more nuanced skills, and although we all have varying degrees of ability when it comes to negotiation, we can always improve. Perhaps you are great at negotiating contracts with vendors, but when it comes to getting what you want out of a colleague, you fall flat. Maybe you can get your kids to go to bed when you say so or get the entire family to agree with you on a vacation spot, but when it comes to grappling with senior management you're paralyzed. Remember, you're the director, so you have to achieve your goals in a variety of environments. But how?

The first step is to remind yourself that flipping is all about your needs, your wants, and your goals. I've spent a lot of time in this book underscoring that point—because it is an essential mind-set in making your flip—so that is what the next section is about. So say it with me: I am in the director's chair!

IT REALLY IS ALL ABOUT ME!

Over the years I'm sure we've all had occasional petty arguments with our spouses, friends, or family. Though I hope that I'm not revealing too much about my own faults and failings, one recurring theme that I've begun to notice in my arguments and the fights of others I've overheard is the following comment: "You're so selfish. It's all about you and what you want." I've been struck by what a silly argument that is—because it *is* all about you in the end. When someone says this, he or she doesn't seem to understand that almost all of us are motivated by what is good for *us*—and that doesn't mean you're an insensitive jerk. We're all motivated by self-interest. What sets people apart, and what will allow you to get what you want, is how you behave in the pursuit of getting your way. As I was thinking about how I would present my ideas on negotiation, I was struck by an image I'd seen. Recently, on the cover of the fashion magazine *W,* the editor had cleverly placed a photo of the reality star Kim Kardashian in the nude, except for three strips of lettering created by the pop artist Barbara Kruger that concealed her delicate areas. The strips were placed across each part of Kardashian's private anatomy, and they read as follows:

It's all about me.
I mean you.
I mean me.

Ms. Kruger has built her career on such simple but telling insights into the relationship between feminism and consumerism by creating art that juxtaposes words and images. It was a smart and ironic take on the state of celebrity and success in the United States—and thinking in this way can help you as you work to become a better negotiator. It really is all about you, but you want to make other parties think it's about them, so that you can get what you want and ultimately have it be about you. Make sense? Trust me, it will.

I've organized my ten rules of negotiation into three separate subsections:

1. Internal negotiation: It's about me.
2. External negotiation: It's about the other person.
3. Tactics of successful negotiation: It's about me again.

The first step when starting any negotiation is to get yourself mentally organized and prepared to go to the table. To do this, begin by creating a clear and actionable game plan, beginning with asking yourself: What is it I want? What do I want to accomplish to make the communication or meeting constructive? What does success look like? What do I want to walk away with? It's essential to have a clear opening position as well as know what you're trying to get out of the negotiation. Establishing this position means that you can see both the obstacles and goals with clarity. Think about how you can communicate your wants to the other party definitively and how to frame them as objectively as possible. The proper phrasing and presentation of information are critical at this stage. Yet being objective can be one of the biggest challenges to overcome. For instance, when stating your opening position, a mistake I see all the time is that the goal may be open to interpretation or ambiguous. Here are a couple of examples of what I'm talking about:

A. In motivating an employee: "You need to be more proactive."

B. In seeking better communication with one's partner: "I feel like you don't listen to me."

OPENING THE NEGOTIATION

When opening a negotiation, each of these statements and ones like them can be a potential land mine and move you farther away from your flip. The problem is that opening statements can't be too ambiguous and rely on the other person's perspective for an answer or definition. There's just too much room for personal interpretations. When you open a negotiation, you need to limit interpretation and stay focused on your goal. Consider examples A and B:

Example A

If the goal is to motivate employees on your team by telling them to be more proactive, you have to define "proactive." I would bet that most employees think they *are* being proactive and doing a good job, which is the reason they're doing things a certain way in the first place. A better way to illustrate your goal could be "I like what you're doing. To take it to a new level, we need to increase your execution on projects. Two things that would help us do that would be to increase sales volume by ten percent and give me four new account leads a month." The point here is to be as specific as possible. If you have observed behavior that undermines the employee's results, identify it and suggest ways to change those actions. You could say, "I realize that you are spending more than the required eight hours in the office and that you come in around 7 A.M. and leave around 4 P.M., but you do have a lot of clients on the West Coast and you're leaving just as their workday gets fully under way. I'd like to see you devote two days a week to a more conventional workday for our office, maybe try 10 A.M. to 6 P.M. and see if that makes a difference."

Example B

Another example of how you can better open a more productive negotiation is moving away from "feeling" words to action words. For example, when someone says, "I feel like you don't listen to me," he or she is making a charged statement. It sounds more like a demand and indictment than a goal for improved communication. A more productive opening could be "I'd really like to figure out a way we could both feel comfortable sharing our thoughts with each other." This comes across in a way that suggests a working partnership. Negotiating for what you want in a personal relationship is much more complex than in business scenarios. You or your spouse, parent, or sibling has baggage that has taken decades to collect, while work colleagues have baggage, too; with personal issues, you can't walk away from the situation and go home for the evening, as you can when dealing with a work situation. In those instances, you will probably need to deploy all of the behavioral and negotiation techniques I've covered in this book. Certainly, the tools in this chapter will help you immensely.

Now that you're at the table—you've delivered your opener and presented what you want in a clear, objective manner—it's time to use the following rules to help keep you on track as you negotiate to get what you want. These are the ten rules you need to know. I've divided them into subsections under the three main negotiation parts of this chapter:

1. Internal Negotiation (It's About Me)
   Rule 1. Understand that it's not personal.
   Rule 2. Take a stand.
   Rule 3. Be a control freak.
2. External Negotiation (It's About the Other Person)
   Rule 4. Keep things objective.
   Rule 5. Be realistic.
   Rule 6. Remember that you have two ears and one mouth.
   Rule 7. Recognize the power of silence.
3. Tactics of Successful Negotiation (It's About Me Again)
   Rule 8. Prove it.
   Rule 9. Become entitled.
   Rule 10. Be aware of your body language.

1. INTERNAL NEGOTIATION (IT'S ABOUT ME)

Rule 1: Understand that it's not personal.

This may be the hardest thing to do. You can't help but bring your own feelings, fears, and issues along for the ride, but the more you can see things objectively, the better your chances of moving the ball forward. Imagine if each football player on a team's offensive line took the aggressive tactics of the defensive line of the opposing team personally. He might imagine that his opponents were all trying to attack him and purposely hurt him rather than understanding their objective reality: to score points. The football player has to realize that it's not about him. The defensive line has a job to do, which is to stop the ball from moving down the field. It's not a personal issue on either side, but each is dealing with players who are an obstacle to their goal. Now, I'm sure a lot of you are thinking about the brawls you've seen break out on the field every now and then. Well, I guess those guys may have taken it personally—but unfortunately this often results in fouls, fines, and ejections. How can you avoid having your flip called foul or, worse yet, being ejected from the game?

The thing to keep in mind is that it's just business. I've seen enough deals brokered between individuals who under other circumstances could barely speak to each other. But if the deal made good business sense, they figured out a way to communicate and make the deal. You don't have to hate your opponent to win, but you don't have to think of him as your best friend either. You want to establish an environment and dynamic that supports direct, constructive communication. Keep your wants, as well as those of the other party, in mind. In any negotiation, spend less time worrying about being liked and more time being fair, and never take personal shots.

Likewise, don't waste energy feeling personally put upon: try to look at things from the defensive line's position. What are the objectives of the other party, and how can you get yours to align with theirs so you can move your agenda forward? In a previous chapter I mentioned the book *Getting to Yes,* which addresses one of the foundational concepts of successful negotiations, "principled" negotiating. With this approach, you keep the mutual principles of both parties in mind and work toward achieving those goals. Though you of course want to win, this is not about beating up the other guy. A win or loss isn't personal; it's what gets you closer to your mutual goal. You can control only your own actions, and there will be times when the other person will stoop to a personal level. The only thing to do in that case is to take the high road. Do not engage. This is a key negotiation tactic. It may be difficult to do, but the moral high ground always provides the best view.

Rule 2: Take a stand.

In 1957 Ayn Rand published a novel entitled *Atlas Shrugged,* the main theme of which serves our purpose. One of the book's primary concepts is that the leading innovators, people who come up with new ideas and whom today we refer to as "intellectual capital," refuse to be exploited by society, preferring to benefit from their own efforts. But when the government becomes more and more involved with private businesses and industry, society begins to collapse. With all of this government control, society's most productive citizens begin to disappear, one by one. They are led by the mysterious figure John Galt, whose movement is meant to stop "the motor of the world" by withdrawing its best minds, thereby leaving the government with no way to keep society going.

I refer to this story in describing rule 2 because it demonstrates the idea that you have to be prepared to walk away from any negotiation in which you feel the other party is being unreasonable or overly controlling or taking advantage of you. Learn to walk away, and don't succumb to another person's exploitation; that is what I consider taking a stand. I realize that taking a stand and being prepared to walk away in any negotiation is easier said than done, but you can do it if you believe in your worth and bide your time in terms of reaching an agreement. It goes back to understanding that unfortunately, both in business and in life, many people have to lose something before they can see its value. I have experienced this many times in my career. I've witnessed employees who can't seem to get promoted in their companies, only to find, when they leave the company and begin working elsewhere, that their former employers offer to rehire the person for greater responsibility. In such cases, I have to admit, my advice has been to pull back. If you feel you are overworked, for example, don't agree to take on any more additional assignments unless the company plans to compensate you fairly or provides you with additional support.

That doesn't necessarily mean that you should end a relationship or kill an opportunity for good, but it could mean that you should take a time-out or employ the strategic anger technique I talked about earlier. You need to reestablish your worth to the company, and taking a stand can help. In the case of a boss who is constantly throwing new projects at you but vetoing your decisions regarding those projects, you can call that to his attention, saying "You know, my accounts have made the company $4 million in the last year, but right now my compensation does not reflect those contributions. I think before I agree to take on more, I'd like to discuss how you view my role in this department." You're not being insubordinate and you're not reacting emotionally, you're just stating that you feel as though you're not being valued even though all the evidence shows that you are adding value to the company's bottom line. Though it may sound risky to stand up for yourself openly, remember that it's never what you say, it's how you say it. So don't accuse, inquire. Ask your boss for more information to open the negotiation.

 Flip Tip: Don't accuse, inquire.

A colleague once told me a story about how her boss was consistently making decisions about her product line without consulting her. She confronted him, saying "I want to take responsibility for my business, but I find it challenging if I am not informed of all the decisions." She stood up for herself but put the ball back into his court: "Can you recommend a way we can work together better?" She had opened the negotiations by stating her position firmly yet respectfully. What she found out was that her boss hadn't even realized he was cutting her out of the loop. Rather than being upset that she stood her ground, he was apologetic and they were able to come to a mutual agreement about how to handle decisions going forward.

Rule 3: Be a control freak.

With the understanding that criticism or obstacles are not personal and the knowledge that you have the power to walk away, the next technique you'll need to master is control. In the next paragraphs I'll show you how to learn to control your emotions and manage other people's to your advantage.

Earlier in this chapter, I told you how important it is to establish a game plan before entering into any kind of negotiation. Part of that plan is to examine your emotions concerning the upcoming conversation. What do you feel, and what emotions do you want to project to the other party? Are you at the point of being so impatient with the other individual that you aren't willing to have a conversation and just want to tell him the way things are going to be? If that's the case, take a deep breath and think rationally. Are you really going to get what you want by making loud demands? Ideally, you'll go to the negotiation feeling confident about your position yet open-minded about other possible solutions. The first step is to examine how you feel compared to how you want to feel. Then you need to try to figure out the same thing about the opposing party. What is that person's emotional state? You may also want to think about where the opposing party might *want* to be emotionally.

After you identify your emotions, the next step is to figure out why you're feeling them. Are you nervous because you know that you're going to have a confrontation and you're just not wired that way? Or are you anxious because you know your manager really wants this contract to happen—on her terms, of course—and you don't want to deal with the ramifications of not succeeding or having to make too many concessions? And what about the other person?

One way to keep things constructive and moving forward is to question the other person's emotions as they emerge during the negotiation. Perhaps you're meeting with a client who has an endless list of complaints and grievances he wants to get through before you address the matter at hand. Rather than trying to dissuade him from saying his piece and making excuses for his bad experience, just listen. You don't have to agree that he was the wronged party, especially if it hurts your negotiating position, but it doesn't hurt to let him get his feelings out into the open and hopefully have some cathartic release. You can use comments such as "I see that you're upset," "I can understand that you're frustrated," or "Let's agree to acknowledge that your office was left unsatisfied about our service." By doing this you can accomplish three things:

1. You let the other party express his or her emotions so that they don't continue to cloud future dealings.

2. You gain that person's trust because by listening you legitimize his or her feelings; you listen even though you don't necessarily agree.

3. You can spin the current negotiation in your favor by refining your position to address the person's complaints.

If someone is so emotional that he begins yelling or saying completely irrational things, you should table the conversation to a later time and remove yourself from the meeting physically. You could say something such as "Why don't we break for lunch and resume our conversation later in the day?" or "Perhaps we should talk later, when we've all had some time to consider."

My last piece of advice on this topic is that the better you are in control of yourself, the more you can take advantage of an opposing party who is acting irrationally—whether authentically or as some kind of negotiating posture.

2. EXTERNAL NEGOTIATION (IT'S ABOUT THE OTHER PERSON)

In any negotiation, after you have stated your desires, you need to ask yourself, what does the other party want? So far you've established what you think is the opposing person's mental or emotional state and established a sense of trust; how can you keep that momentum going by appealing to that person's needs and goals in order to come to a negotiated solution that still meets your primary objective? The next four rules will help you in this effort.

Rule 4: Keep things objective.

Keeping an objective perspective on others' motives is essential in helping you get the right information and feedback before you enter into a negotiation or difficult conversation. As you investigate the motives, emotions, and needs of the other party, are you bringing in the opinions of others? If so, who do you have in your peanut gallery?

Professional circles are often small, which can make getting objective feedback difficult. A cross section of your colleagues will likely have either extremely positive or irrationally negative things to say, such as "So-and-so is a terrible communicator. He ignored my email for at least a week" or "Margaret is a wonderful employee. I hired her ten years ago and am very impressed by her work ethic." Do you really think someone who has a vested interest in the success or failure of another colleague is going to be objective?

You have to weed out both extremes when conducting due diligence. And when an opposing party confronts you with evidence of his or her worth and value by citing the opinion of someone close to him or her, you have to nip it in the bud. If someone says, "My friend from editing really liked my article" or "I showed my boyfriend, Hugh, the article I wrote, and he loved it," be ready to respond with an opinion that is objective and constructive. For example, "Well, I shared your article with a developmental editor, and he thought that we could punch it up a bit—with more active sentences, perhaps."

Let's take this idea a bit further and imagine that you are going to have to negotiate for what you want and for what you feel your client wants in a meeting with an advertising art director. In this scenario you are an account manager at an ad agency. You've worked hard and developed what you feel will be an impressive advertising campaign. You have met with the clients, and you know that the clients like your ideas. You have a vision of what you want the ad to look like. You turn over your client notes and ideas to the agency's creative team to bring your vision to life. The problem is that what is placed in front of you in the meeting is an ad campaign that only vaguely resembles your ideas. The art director and creative team have completely changed your ideas, and from what you know their ideas will be off base to the clients.

The conversation could go something like this:

Art director: Don't these ads look amazing?

You: Wow, tell me how you got to this place; it feels very different from what we originally talked about.

Art director: Yeah, thanks. You know, we thought about some of the things you said, but the team really liked this new direction, it feels fresh to us.

You: While I understand your team said they liked that design direction, you are really the lead art director. Do you think the clients are going to respond as favorably?

Art director: Look, we're the creatives. They hire us to be creative. It's our job to lead them. You've got to sell them on why this idea is better.

You: I agree, you and your team have been really creative here, but I honestly have to feel that this is a better idea before I can stand behind it. While I like that your team really was inspired, we need to stay focused on the original objective. Let's do this: I would rather share these ads with some other people on the team and bring feedback so we can discuss next steps further.

To win here, you need to take the emotion out of the conversation by using feedback from outside sources that are as objective as possible. Keep your negotiations as objective as possible to gain credibility and persuasion.

Rule 5: Be realistic.

Too many times I've seen deals go south because one side created an expectation that was unrealistic and had no flexibility to accommodate any sort of compromise. So, rather than moving forward, the deal just died. You have to think like the famed Fidelity stockbroker Peter Lynch. He said he had made most of his money by selling his stocks early, when it had achieved moderate gains, rather than assuming that a stock would continue to increase in value. The same rule applies when negotiating.

It would be a mistake to enter any negotiation with the belief that you're going to get 100 percent of what you want and will have to give nothing to the other party. That's not going to happen, and one of the timeworn rules of negotiating is to leave something on the table for the other guy. This makes a lot of sense, particularly if you have an ongoing relationship with the other party. Plus, it puts into action your commitment to think about what is mutually acceptable. This will certainly help you in the long run as you continue to deal with the person.

But being realistic doesn't mean that you *have* to make unwanted concessions—and you certainly don't want to enter a negotiation with defeat in mind or a plan to back down without a strong reason. What it does mean is that in addition to knowing what your walkaway point is, you should consider the next best alternatives to what you're asking for. As you prepare for any negotiation, keep those alternatives in mind.

Every year in the fall, magazines start developing their business plans for the upcoming business year. It is the time of year when many magazines begin long negotiations with their largest advertisers. Big multinational companies use their potential advertising revenue commitments to press for the most favorable rates, positioning within the magazine (far-forward positions are the most valuable), and something in the industry called "added value," which could be anything from events that a magazine sets up on behalf of the advertiser to online digital projects to additional exposure within the magazine. They pit magazines against one another to strengthen their negotiating position: *US Weekly* versus *People* or *Glamour* versus *InStyle*. If a magazine asks for too much in terms of page and revenue commitments, they may go to a competitor. If it asks for too little or gives away the store to secure the business, its bottom line may be compromised.

In such a case—and similar situations crop up in many different industries—you need to use Rule 5 and be realistic to win. To be realistic, create a threshold in your mind that you will not go below. It is the place where you feel, when you walk away from the negotiations, that if you achieved it you would be satisfied. In terms of baseball, it would be a double. Look, you can swing for the fences, but your chance of hitting a home run, as in baseball, is rare. Once you determine that place, ask for 20 percent more, knowing that you will have to give a little and come down in the negotiations. Doing so will leave both parties walking away feeling good.

Rule 6: Remember that you have two ears and one mouth.

Listening effectively is one of your most important assets when negotiating. Remember: you have two ears and one mouth, so you should listen twice as much as you speak. What does it mean to listen, exactly? Hearing isn't listening. If you're reviewing your notes or thinking about your next meeting or the silly thing your mother said to you on the phone last night, you may be aware of the words being spoken, but you're not concentrating on their content or context. You're also disrespecting the other person, and that won't help you as your discussion continues.

Listening takes several forms. There's passive listening, which I referred to earlier in this chapter, in which you let the other party voice his or her feelings and opinions. When you're listening passively, you don't need to really say anything, but you do need to listen intently. By paying close attention to another party's speech, you are showing him that you care about his opinion, and, more important, you can mine what he says for clues that will help you in the negotiation. You can also better gauge the other person's emotions and listen for information that may have been unavailable to you up until now—insider stuff, perhaps.

When you practice acknowledgment as you listen, whether through speech or action, you are validating, though not necessarily agreeing with, the other person's statements. You can respond with visual cues—nodding your head in agreement, looking skeptical if you disagree—or offer comments such as "I see how you can feel that way," "Tell me more about that experience," or "Dealing with that vendor must've been frustrating." But the most beneficial approach is active listening. When you listen actively, you embed yourself in the conversation and jump in at critical points, either to get more information that will help you refine your own position or to nip some irrational demand in the bud. Active listening is an opportunity for both parties to refine their positions—by putting the brakes on unreasonable requests before they get too far and thinking of alternatives as each becomes more aware of what the other party is looking for.

Before I get into the steps that inform effective active listening, we should spend a minute discussing some of the traps you will want to avoid.

1. *Listening means actually "listening."* When trying to explain the value of active listening, I remember an old saying I used to hear growing up: "God gave you two ears and one mouth." This means you should listen twice as much as you talk. When managing any negotiation, it's simple: listen twice as much as you talk. You will be amazed when you close your mouth and open your ears how much information the other party gives you.

2. *Know your audience.* Are the points you are trying to make valuable and relevant to the person across the table. People often ignore what they don't want to hear; make certain what you are saying matters to them.

3. *Are you listening or waiting to speak?* Often in any negotiation, each side enters the discussion with a mental list of points or ideas that they want to get across. The trouble is, a good negotiation is dynamic, like a game of tennis. It changes with every ball hit across the net. If you are just waiting to speak then you aren't listening.

With these pitfalls in mind, below is the top five list of best advice for active listening that negotiation coaches advise you should develop:

1. *Do Your Homework.* Information is power. Think about it: good negotiations are like good business plans— they're built on solid information and research. The more information and research you've done ahead of time the better prepared you'll be and the more successful the outcome.

2. *Have an Agenda.* Once you have completed your research create an agenda with specific goals you wish to achieve. Know what is it you want to get out of the discussion. Consider primary goals as well as fall back positions. Creating fallback positions allows you room to navigate during the negotiation and concede some points.

3. *Ask Questions.* Have you ever seen a really good television interview? Have you ever seen a really bad one? There is much to be learned from watching a seasoned pro like Diane Sawyer at work. Success does not come from the number of questions asked. Success comes about asking the *right* questions. The questions that provide you with the information you need. Your questions should have two goals: (1) to gather specific information to your situation, and (2) to find out what their goals and needs are. Questions should be asked strategically, starting with the most general questions and ending with the most specific.

4. *Take Notes.* Write it down. Write it down. Write it down. While many of us believe that we can remember what has been said, often while we are in the middle of any negotiation this is not the case. Both parties will remember slightly different versions of events. The more information you write down the more credibility, insight, and power you can gain in that moment and in the future if the negotiations continue on.

5. *Watch and Learn.* Always allow the other party to start first. Good negotiation is like a tennis game. You react individually to each ball that is hit over the net to you. When you let the other party begin first you will have the best understanding of what their goals and agendas are. Letting your colleague speak first also provides you with the most amount of time to think and prepare to hit the ball back. Each time they speak and finish their thoughts. Use the three-second rule. Once they have finished speaking, allow for three seconds of silence. The three

seconds of silence allows you to reflect on what has been said, it also allows you to look for nonverbal clues. Does what he/she is saying match up with how they are sitting, or the look in their eyes, or their facial expressions?

A great example of how active listening benefited a negotiation occurred years ago, when I made the leap from salesperson to manager. My old boss called me up to meet for breakfast. She had recently been promoted from a magazine where we had worked together into a publisher's position at another magazine. When we met, she said, "I really enjoyed working together, come work for me." As I had been in a sales position for only a year, my assumption was that with my limited experience she wanted me to move over to her magazine in a sales capacity. And quite honestly, I loved working with her and would have made the jump into a lateral position right then and there. But here's where the active listening really worked; rather than speaking that day and filling in the blanks, I just smiled, nodded, and said nothing. I let her finish what she was saying.

She continued, "I have to rebuild the team. I could really use people that know my work style." I nodded again. I didn't cut in and tell her why I would be so right for a position; rather, I asked a question to get more information: "So what do you need?" I was still assuming that she was going to ask me to take over a sales list, but I wanted to hear it from her. She responded, "I need great salespeople, and I need a better management team." Her body language changed; it became more open, and she leaned forward. She went on to explain her challenges and how finding people who "got" her hard-charging management approach was difficult. Again I nodded; through active listening I could see that she had many challenges and needs. I started to think that maybe there was a larger role I could play in her organization than just sales. When she finished, I helped set the stage by saying "I'm completely happy where I am but loved working together with you. A jump like this is exciting but has its risks. I guess it all depends on career growth and what role you think I can play."

She thought and asked, "What about a management position?"

If I had not used active listening and had spoken too quickly at the beginning of the conversation, I might not be writing this book today. Try it, it works.

Rule 7: Recognize the power of silence.

Hand in hand with the ability to listen is the power of silence. There are times during a conversation when not responding is your best course of action. Negotiation experts agree that silence can be your most powerful tool. It does one of three things:

1. It leaves open a gap that your counterpart is compelled to fill with information that you can use to your advantage.
2. It signals your displeasure with what is being proposed. I like adding a flinch to signal displeasure, as well. This tends to take the wind out of the other person's sails and gives you a bargaining advantage.
3. It buys you time to think in a situation where your counterpart is asking or acting in a way you hadn't considered. You'll gain important moments to think about the impact of what he's asking and maybe the chance to come up with a few alternatives.

Of these three, the most effective use of silence is when you combine it with listening, so that you can mine previously undisclosed information from your counterpart. Some people just can't stand a silent pause and feel compelled to fill it. It's during such periods, when the opposing party is nervously gabbing away, that you can get more insight—from what he's saying, his tone of voice, and nonverbal cues. If you know that you're dealing with such a person, you should initiate the silence, if possible. However, what if your counterpart also likes to make use of silence or doesn't respond? One way to get things back on track is to turn your silence into a thoughtful pause. Break the silence with a leading but noncommittal remark: "That's interesting" or "Really" or "I'll have to think about that."

The point is that you want to combine your listening skills with the understanding that silence can be an important weapon in achieving what you want from the negotiation. This can work in any situation. Think about the email demands you get. Do you respond right away? Next time, let the email sit a day and see if the person has a change of heart about what he really needs and when. Being overly responsive either verbally or via written communication can be detrimental to your cause.

3. TACTICS OF SUCCESSFUL NEGOTIATION (IT'S ABOUT YOU AGAIN)

Now we're back to you and what you want out of the negotiation. You've listened to your counterpart and have a sense of where he's coming from, but now you need to push your position forward as you planned or readjust it based on any new information you have received and present the new plan to the other person. Here are the final three rules you need to follow.

Rule 8: Prove it.

As any good lawyer knows, feelings or perceptions don't win cases; proof does. When you enter into any type of negotiation, you need to bring as much evidence to the table as possible. Whether it's your reluctance to let your teenager spend a night at a friend's house or your request for a raise, you have to prove your point. In addition to embodying the skills we've already covered, you need to have the facts of the case at your fingertips.

When I say "facts," I mean it. It's not enough to tell your manager how hard you work, that you spend nights and weekends on your projects, and that you devote yourself to your job. That just makes it sound as if you can't get your work done in the eight hours a day you're being paid for. A sounder argument is to cite the revenue or revenue opportunities you've brought to the firm. For example: "I've made my sales goal three years straight, and I'm the only one in our department to have accomplished this" or "The associates on our team often approach me for advice, and in fact I've been having weekly informal sessions with them to teach them the ins and outs of our business."

Have the facts in hand, and use them to make your point. Bosses can't argue with results, and you can't sugarcoat or spin your inability to meet your goals. Before considering any negotiation, look at yourself—warts and all—and determine how much bargaining power you have based on your results. If you're being unfairly kept in a certain position because of a misperception, hit 'em with the facts—numbers don't lie.

Rule 9: Become entitled.

I used to start every negotiation by preparing myself mentally. Whenever I needed to raise my expectations and block out all my insecurities, I would allow myself to think over and over about all the ways I was getting "screwed." What I really needed to do was find the moral high ground and the fortitude to become my own best advocate. Here's how I used this conviction effectively when I was looking for my first sales position.

At the time I had no sales experience. I interviewed at several places and was eventually offered an "internal sales" position, which meant phone sales. The human resources person told me I was lucky to get the spot and should take it. She went on to persuade me that I had no experience and the position would provide me with the experience I needed to get the job I really wanted. Her argument made some sense, and it was tempting. But I remember thinking that I deserved better, even though it probably didn't look that way on paper. I didn't want to be selling on the phone, I wanted to be out on the street. So I told her that I would not take the job, that I believed in myself and was ready for an outside sales job. She was flabbergasted and told me she thought I might regret my decision.

As it turned out, I did secure an outside sales position at the New York Times Magazine group. I was offered a position selling the health and beauty aids list for *Child* magazine. The smart, seasoned advertising director believed that she could channel my ambitions, so she gave me a shot. Then, six months later, the original HR person who had told me I might regret my decision called me. She was now working for my current employer, and even though, she said, she thought I was arrogant, she might have a better position than my current spot for me. This story shows that the greatest value of becoming entitled in a negotiation is the understanding that not all negotiations have an expiration date. Walking away at the moment is just that: a moment. The act of sometimes leaving the opposition wanting more can be one of your greatest assets, but you have to have self-conviction and act accordingly. The footnote to that story is that I have worked happily for the company for seventeen years.

Rule 10: Be aware of your body language.

Along with what you say, you communicate a lot with nonverbal gestures and expressions. There are two reasons you need to understand body language in negotiations: to be aware of the signals you are sending and to be able to read the signals that are being sent to you.

THE SIGNALS YOU SEND

In this chapter I have outlined a few techniques you can use to your advantage when discussing what you want with your counterpart. Maintaining eye contact and controlling your hand gestures and fidgeting are key to exuding confidence. Techniques you can use to convey that you are taking in every word the other person is saying include leaning forward, nodding, and suggesting with your facial expressions that you are considering his or her every word. When sitting at the negotiation table, it is important to sit tall and hold your hands down, off the table. When you place your hands with your palms down, you signal authority and control. If during the process you need time to think, a good technique to buy time is something called "steepling." Used correctly, steepling, or putting your fingertips together to form a "church steeple," can show that you are confident and thoughtfully considering what the other party is saying. The most recognizable bad example of steepling is the gesture regularly performed by Mr. Burns of *The Simpsons* fame. The action is part of what makes the character funny—in his case the reason it undermines his credibility is that he combines the gesture with negative body language, such as slouching and grimacing. To use steepling effectively, lean forward, then bring your hands up to the base of your chin. The body language message delivered is that of thoughtful contemplation.

THE SIGNALS OTHER PEOPLE SEND

When assessing body language and the messages being sent to you, it's important to consider the age and gender of the person involved. Age, culture, and gender can all affect body language. Older executives tend to be more modest in their body language, while younger men are more energetic. But there are some basic body messages that are consistent across all groups. Crossed arms indicate being defensive or bored. Adjusting cuffs, watch, or tie can mean nervousness. When one's palms are up, it signifies openness and a desire to communicate. Touching the nose can mean dishonesty or exaggeration. A hand supporting the chin or face can mean boredom, and taking off glasses usually signifies that the person is ready to speak. Understanding and reading nonverbal clues can be a great asset as you work on your flip.

• • •

Keep in mind all you've gained by going through these steps: you've come to a negotiation with a plan in place, you're mentally and emotionally prepared, you've created an environment in which your counterpart believes you are considering what is mutually beneficial, and you're saying the right, factually supported things when presenting your case. Now you have an advantage by suggesting, through body language, that you are in control and deserve to be in the power seat. As I said at the beginning of the chapter, this is your show, and you are the writer, actor, and director all wrapped up in one.

I've covered all aspects of the flip in these nine chapters, from how to develop the belief and confidence that you deserve better opportunities to the tools for making your flip happen. Now I'll wrap it up in the next and final chapter by talking about managing setbacks, building on your flips, and the most important aspect of flipping successfully: turning intention into action.

Chapter 9

Now It's Up to You

A successful person is one who can lay a firm foundation
with the bricks that others throw at him or her.

—DAVID BRINKLEY

I'M NOT REALLY a procrastinator by nature, but somehow I've found
myself really struggling to sit down and write this last chapter. When
I think about it, though, my aversion to endings makes sense. I have
to be honest: at most of the parties I attend I sneak out without telling the host I'm leaving. I assure myself that my intentions are good,
that my motivation is simply not to interrupt the flow of the party
by signaling my departure, but, in reality I guess at the core I've always hated good-byes. And this chapter is a good-bye of sorts. I think
that's why I've managed to write only nine chapters; ten feels so finite,
and who knows, maybe there will be a sequel. Even finishing chapter
9 felt like an ending, and maybe that's why I find myself willing to do
just about anything else, including going through that old box of pa-
pers I haven't looked at in years, rather than sitting down to write it.
So, just as in my story about my friend who convinced herself that she
lost her cell phone so she wouldn't call her insensitive boyfriend, I am
going to redirect my thinking. Rather than seeing this final chapter
as a good-bye, I choose to see it as a new beginning for each person
reading this book.

Think of this as the first chapter in your personal story. I'm hope-
ful that you've been able to take something positive away from the

experience of learning to flip the script. I assure you that it can work for you. If I were asked, "What is the most important thing I'd like every person to take away from reading this book?" I would answer that no matter who you are and no matter what your circumstances, you have the power and ability to make changes for the better—if you want to. You can write the happy ending you deserve. *Why not you?* The feeling of freedom caused by breaking old patterns and the success and liberation resulting from it can be life-changing.

And although I'd like to fool myself into believing that you devoured every word I wrote, the truth is that we remember only a fraction of what we read. I will assume that you may have forgotten some points discussed earlier in the book, from the first chapters, which focused on understanding so that you can build a sense of self-awareness, to the middle of the book, which focused on strategies for mapping your script and sticking to the plan, to the final third, on how to navigate and win through methods and skill sets that build your ability to intuit a situation, shape it to your needs, and negotiate an outcome that is in your favor. In this chapter I want to recap some of the key principles and outline a cheat sheet to flipping your script.

Flipping isn't about being perfect; we're human, and making mistakes is part of the process of learning and changing. You have to give yourself some room to strike out from time to time and be able to laugh at yourself and understand that changing your life, improving your career, or reaching your goals is going to be full of twists and turns, steps forward, and stumbles backward. With all this in mind, I'd like to discuss maintaining a positive attitude as you encounter setbacks—as you surely will—in attempting to flip your script.

ONE FLIP CAN LEAD TO ANOTHER

How can you learn to keep a positive attitude even in the face of setbacks? How can you discover that one flip can lead to another? Learning to laugh at yourself is really one of the best ways. Whenever I'm interviewing someone, I always think, does this person build himself up to seem perfect and infallible, or when she tells a story, does she reveal her flaws and have the ability to laugh at herself and see the humor in even the most trying circumstances? If the latter, my opinion is the person is probably better adjusted and self-confident than his or her supposedly perfect competitor. It is the self-confident, secure person who can reveal his or her tender underbelly and still exude professionalism.

I have had so many embarrassing situations in my career, and many of them are tied to flips. An example of this comes courtesy of one of my primary Alpha Flips. At one point, my Alpha Flip was to move ahead in my career, be promoted, and become the publisher of the magazine at which I was working. I was still young, but I had a driving ambition and I was determined to reach my goal. To achieve it, I broke the larger flip down into five smaller flips. One of the smaller flips was to increase my efficiency, meaning that I wanted to maximize the volume of work I did in a day. That was a shortsighted idea, because although I became the king of moving the most work, issues, and problems from my inbox to my outbox, what I was gaining in efficiency, I was losing in likability. I was achieving success and being noticed by my superiors in all the right ways, but I was fearful that I was losing my personal touch with my team. I didn't spend any extra time chatting or getting to know them better on a personal level. Whereas today I have completely changed my opinion about what success at work means, at the time I was just beginning to realize that I needed their support and my desire to be only work-focused was taking precedence over taking a few extra seconds to ask people how their weekend had been or inquire about the impact of dropping their oldest child off at college or even about the cold they'd been fighting. And I didn't feel good about it.

I needed to add a new flip to the old one. What was suffering in the process of my becoming more efficient was what had helped to make me successful in the first place—that I was a bit irreverent and created a strong connection with my team and clients. With that in mind I endeavored to create a new flip for myself. It would be about taking the time to stop, ask about others, and regain my personal touch—to be empathetic.

With this fresh in my mind, I disciplined myself to slow down, focus on whomever I was talking to, and ask questions. Within just a few weeks, I saw that it was working. I discovered a newfound sense of pride in my ability to connect and create an empathetic bond with whomever I was speaking. And I was still keeping my efficiency at a high level. I was so proud, maybe too proud. I felt like Jack Dawson in the movie *Titanic* when he proclaimed himself "king of the world." But remember what happened to the *Titanic*? Any sense of foreboding, however, had no effect on me when I was feeling so supremely confident.

KEEP LAUGHING

I remember one spring afternoon: I was walking from our offices in the Times Square area of New York City to meet the president of a company I was trying to impress. We were in the process of wooing him and his high-fashion company to do business with my magazine. He was reluctant, and I needed to show him how much of a player I was and therefore why he should trust me when I told him that my magazine would be the right place for him to advertise.

I decided we would have lunch at a fashionable hangout for media movers and shakers. The restaurant, Michael's, is located in midtown Manhattan, and it's the type of place you go to be seen. It is not unusual on any given day to see Barbara Walters at one table, Mayor Michael Bloomberg sitting close by, and Nelson Mandela around the corner.

This was going to be my day; I was unstoppable. I felt I had my magic touch back; I was efficient *and* empathetic. I could feel the confidence exuding from me with every step I took. I looked good striding down the street with the warm smell of spring in the air, smiling at those walking by. I had the feeling that at any moment I could stop a passerby, reach out and touch her on the sleeve, look deeply into her eyes, and she would immediately understand that I—and only I— could help her.

On this day, I was going to show that fashion president how success was done. I practically flung the door to the restaurant open. I could see that he was standing there in front of the hostess. "Bob!" I cried. I threw out an arm and grasped his hand with a firm but friendly handshake. I was wondering if he could feel the power. Did he know he was having lunch with Mr. Empathy? "Wackermann," I said to the hostess in a confident tone. "Yes, Mr. Wackermann, right this way." "After you, Bob," I invited. "No, after you," he insisted.

"Fine," I thought, "he's going to see me work the room as I led us to our table." I had to show him that I was a player, and here was the perfect opportunity. I quickly scanned the room. Directly in front of me, sitting at a table of three, was a work acquaintance, Jason. He ran a network of city-based publications. Okay, he wasn't Donald Trump, but he would do.

Leading the way into the dining area, I headed straight for Jason and his table, with the fashion president following close behind. To Jason's left was an older gentleman in his midfifties. From his corporate attire, he looked more like a lawyer or accountant than the typical European suit–wearing media type. Sitting directly across from Jason, with his back to me, was a young boy wearing a red baseball hat. "I'll show them how you work a room," I thought.

Before he could respond, I extended my hand to Jason and smiled warmly. "Hey, Jason, how are you doing?" I asked. I was eager to show the fashion president that I had a strong network and could connect with people using my superhuman powers of empathy. Here it was; I wasn't even but a few feet into the space, and already I was bumping into other "players." Jason responded in kind and began to introduce us to his table. But without even breaking eye contact with him, I quickly cut him off. I was the one with the superhuman empathy. I needed to be doing the introductions.

"Jason, this is President X," I said proudly. "Jason," I explained to the president, "is the owner of very successful local media magazines." He seemed impressed. They shook hands. All was going my way. My plan was working perfectly. Now it was time for my coup de grâce. I bent down next to the table in a squatting position, still maintaining eye contact between Jason and President X. Without even looking, I reached out my hand and rested it in a fatherly way on the shoulder of the little boy. In my mind, I thought I was showing the president "See, I'm Mr. Empathy. I can do anything. I can go head-to-head with you, but I've also got the soft touch with the kids. Doesn't that make me great?" So in my best "I feel your preteen angst" tone, I said, gently tapping the boy's shoulder, my smile broadening, "Now, which one of you brought your little son to work?" As the words came out of my mouth, I could immediately see that something was wrong. The look on Jason's face was not the "Wow, isn't Bill so nice" look that I'd been expecting. It was quite another look, one that I'd not seen before. I quickly glanced at the president, as I patted the boy's shoulder again. The president's eyes only grew wider.

I was confused. What was happening? Then I heard the words from Jason's mouth: "Bill, you know Verne, don't you?" Jason cast his eyes down. My head slowly turning, I could feel that the squatting position I had been maintaining on the floor of Michael's was beginning to burn. I turned my head to the left to look at the boy with the red cap. I could feel myself starting to feel a bit weak in the knees. The room started to spin, and for a moment, I experienced the rare case of vertigo that comes only from making a complete fool of yourself.

Verne? As my head made its way around to a complete turn, I found myself staring, not looking at a child, but staring into the annoyed eyes of Verne Troyer, the actor best known for playing Mini-Me in the Austin Powers films. My humiliation was complete. I stayed in my crouched position for what felt like an eternity, speechless. I looked up at the president, who just stood there, eyes cast down. He had the pained expression of someone who had just witnessed a terrible accident. And he had.

There was nothing I could say, and I was so stunned myself that I actually said nothing. I just looked at Verne—and I could see he was pissed. I didn't even muster an apology. Not only had my ego proven that Mr. Empathy was not perfect, it had succeeded in embarrassing me and everyone else at that table. Sometimes in business, there are no words, and that was one of those times. With that unsaid understanding, I just stood up and walked away.

The lunch was a bust. It was tough to recover from my gaffe. The president tried hard to power through lunch as quickly as possible. I think we set a new record of about thirty-eight minutes. We eventually gained advertising from his firm, but only years later, after the president had left the business to run a technology company. I tell this true story to remind people that flipping is an ongoing process. Though you may have good days, prepare for and expect that you'll have some tough ones. Just remember to laugh at the ones that you swear you'll never laugh at, because someday you will. No matter how long I've been doing this and no matter how much advice—good and bad—that I've dished out, there is always room for improvement and growth. There is always another flip I'd like to improve upon. And like our college chemistry class, over time we tend to forget. So here to help you is my Flipping's Top Nine things to remember.

FLIPPING'S TOP NINE

If I had to distill down all the ideas, opinions, experiences, and rules of the past nine chapters, it would be difficult. But I've always been a sucker for lists. Maybe that's why I wound up working in magazine publishing, where the covers of magazines are filled with lists: Top 10 Looks for Fall! 7 Instant Meals! The 50 Sexiest Hotels in the World! So here is my attempt at creating Flipping's Top Nine:

1. Say "So what?" and see what happens.
2. Make room for unplanned good in your life.
3. Have a Plan B, Plan C, Plan D, in case Plan A doesn't work.
4. Blame is like candy; too much is unhealthful and will make you sick.
5. Name your flip; you can have whatever it is you want!

6. Take a stand; stand for something, or fall for everything.
7. Any plan is better than no plan.
8. Take your goals bite by bite; think about them in smaller, manageable bites.
9. Laugh! Everything will be better in the end, and if it's not better, you're not at the end yet. Keep going.

With these nine tips in mind, you need to add fuel to the fire by adding action to your good intentions. Several times throughout this book I talked about the need to act on your ideas or intentions in order to make a change in your life. And I spent a great deal of this book attempting to disable your natural resistance to taking a leap. Do you dream about what life would be like with a promotion but are too intimidated by your boss to make a move? Are you worried to rock the boat with a loved one for fear of doing permanent damage to the relationship? Fear is a natural reaction to change, and it's healthy in that it can keep you from becoming overly confident or arrogant. That said, you still need to muscle past any hesitations you may have that keep you from your flip. You *are* good enough, you *do* deserve happiness and acclaim for your good work, and you *are* entitled to a better station in life. If you can't convince yourself of this, think about all the people in your life who've achieved all of the things that you want for yourself. There is no reason why you don't deserve the same fulfillment. A flip begins with the first step, and remember, it can be a small one. Take a chance on yourself, think about how much better your world would be if a few changes were made, and then create a plan that takes you there. I've given you strategies for examining your interests, strategies for creating a successful flip, and tools for making situations adhere to your needs; now the rest is up to you.

Take that first step, get out that piece of paper, and map out your first flip. I promise you that it will be a liberating step toward an exciting future. With that I am completing what has been one of the most rewarding and challenging flips of my career—this book!

NOTES

CHAPTER 1: THE POWER OF "SO WHAT?"

28   Williams, the author of *Disrupt:* From author's interview with
Luke Williams for this book, September 15, 2010.

CHAPTER 2: RUBY SLIPPERS

43   Billie Jean King: Billie Jean King, *Pressure Is a Privilege: Lessons
I've Learned from Life and the Battle of the Sexes* (New York:
LifeTime Media, 2008), 13.

49   "Personal accountability is about": John G. Miller, *QBQ! The
Question Behind the Question* (New York, Penguin Group, 2004), 59.

CHAPTER 3: "THE BOSS HATES ME" AND OTHER ACTS OF SELF-SABOTAGE

63   "star performance": Daniel Goleman, *Working with Emotional
Intelligence* (New York: Bantam Books, 1998), 32.

63   Here are a few of his findings: Cary Cherniss, "The Business Case
for Emotional Intelligence," prepared for the Consortium for
Research on Emotional Intelligence in Organizations, 1999,
www.eiconsortium.org/pdf/business_case_for_ei.pdf.

75   "the one and only place": Dr. Wayne D. Dyer, *Excuses Begone!:
How to Change Lifelong, Self-Defeating Thinking Habits* (London:
Hay House, 2009), 179.

75   "to live a totally excuse-free life": Ibid.

78   genuine excuse artisans: Benedict Carey, "Some Protect the Ego
by Working on Their Excuses Early," *The New York Times,*
January 9, 2009.

83   "This focus on psychosocial predestination": Raymond Havlicek,
"Is the Good Life Possible After a Bad Childhood?,"
www.drhavlicek.com/articles/index41.htm.

84 "memes are the basic building blocks": www.memecentral.com.

84 "a thought, belief, or attitude": Richard Brodie, *Virus of the Mind: The New Science of the Meme* (London: Hay House, 2009), 125.

89 As a child, Burns: Heidi Evans, "Ursula Burns to Head Xerox, Will Be First Black Woman to Be CEO of Fortune 500 Company," *New York Daily News,* May 22, 2009.

89 "a good education": http://topics.nytimes.com/topics/reference/timestopics/people/b/ursula_m_burns/index.html.

89 "She gave us courage": Ibid.

91 When I was a young boy: Kate Linebaugh and Jane Spencer, "The Revolution of Chairman Li," *The Wall Street Journal,* November 2, 2007.

93 In his book *Hard Optimism:* Price Pritchett, *Hard Optimism: How to Succeed in a World Where Positive Wins* (New York: McGraw-Hill, 2006), 6.

97 If you've caught yourself spiraling: Sue Shellenbarger, "Slumping at Work? What Would Jack Do: How Nicklaus, Other Athletes Can Spark an Office Comeback," *The Wall Street Journal,* October 13, 2010, http://online.wsj.com/article/SB10001424052748704164004575548000174434276.html?KEYWORDS=slump.

CHAPTER 4: THE PROCESS

112 "Goals activate cognitive knowledge": Edwin A. Locke and Gary P. Latham, "Building a Practically Useful Theory of Goal Setting and Task Motivation," *The American Psychologist* 57, no. 9 (September 2002): 705–717.

CHAPTER 5: THE RIGHT THING AND THE HARD THING

125 "What we're really measuring": www.newyorker.com/reporting/2009/05/18/090518fa_fact_lehrer.

CHAPTER 6: STRATEGIC ANGER AND OTHER OFFENSIVE MOVES

146 the act of either concealing: Eduardo B. Andrade and Teck-Hua Ho, "Gaming Emotions in Social Interactions," *Journal of Consumer Research* 36 (December 2009), www.haas.berkeley.edu/faculty/papers/AndradeHo2009.pdf.

146 "The UG can also capture": Ibid.

156 the CRIB method: Kerry Patterson, Joseph Grenny, Ron McMillan, and Al Switzler, *Crucial Conversations* (New York: McGraw-Hill, 2002).

CHAPTER 7: THE ROPE METHOD

160   Consider the old poem: John Godfrey Saxe, "The Blind Men and the Elephant," http://allpoetry.com/poem/8551841-The_Blind_Man_And_The_Elephant-by-John_Godfrey_Saxe.

173   "Three context-specific variables": http://homepages.uwp.edu/crooker/745-Resile/articles/Wanberg-Banas-2000.pdf.

CHAPTER 8: EVERYTHING'S A NEGOTIATION

194   some of the traps you will want to avoid: www.negotiatingguide.com/negotiation/listeningskills.htm.

ACKNOWLEDGMENTS

This book has been an incredible learning experience: getting to 70,000 coherent, organized, and grammatically correct words is more work than you would think! None of it would have been possible without the patience, support, and expertise of people who know and knew much more than I. To that end, there are many people to thank . . . so here I go.

Thank you to Dominick Anfuso, my editor at Free Press, for taking a chance on an unknown "suit" who thought he could be a writer. I hope this book is worthy of your belief in me.

To my agent, Jan Miller, and her business right hand, Shannon Marven, all I can say is "thank you, thank you" for your insights, support, and direction in making this project happen. There would be no *Flip* without you both.

To Samantha Rosenthal, who sitting at lunch one day told me, " I think you should write a book," and set the wheels in motion to help me make it happen. You are my hero.

To everyone at Condé Nast: it is a daily privilege to work at the best content company in the world.

To Matthias Vriens-McGrath for making me look so good. Many thanks.

A massive thank you to my "family" both related and not, for your love, support, and numerous contributions: Ellen, Claire, Jeff, Ed and 2 Boo Productions, Alex, Samantha Roth, Leslie Russo, Mark and Lynn Maltz, Glen and Nancy Fandl, Team Seattle, Donald, Melissa, Joe and Louise, Patrick Connors, Pam Drucker, Bobby Graham, Haley Marks, Chris DiPresso, Maura O'Brien, Jeanne Glasser, Neil Weissman. You have all added something to my life.

INDEX

ABOUT THE AUTHOR

Bill Wackermann is the youngest executive vice president in Condé Nast history, having overseen *Glamour, Brides, Bon Appetit, Details,* and *W* magazines. After joining *Glamour* in April 2004, he implemented a strategy that boosted advertising pages, revenue, profitability, brand vitality, and industry acclaim for the legendary title, which led to his appointment as senior vice president, publishing director in January 2008. In his first year at *Glamour, Crain's New York Business* put Wackermann on its "40 Under 40" list, and in 2005–2006, *Glamour* was named for the first time in its sixty-nine-year history to *Advertising Age's* "A-List" and *Adweek's* "Hot List." Bill has been with Condé Nast for fifteen years. Prior to joining *Glamour,* he was vice president and publisher of *Details,* and before that he was associate publisher at *Condé Nast Traveler.* He has also held sales positions at *Vanity Fair* and *House & Garden.* He is a father of three and a part-time triathlete, and he currently works and lives in New York City.